# GROWING CHILDREN

This edition published in Canada in 2008 by Whitecap Books,
351 Lynn Ave., North Vancouver, British Columbia, Canada, V7J 2C4.
www.whitecap.ca

First published by Murdoch Books Pty Limited in 2008.

Chief Executive: Juliet Rogers
Publishing Director: Kay Scarlett

Design manager: Vivien Valk
Project manager: Colette Vella
Editor: Kim Rowney
Consultant and nutrition analyst: Susanna Holt
Peer review: Carol Fallows
Design concept: Susanne Geppert
Designer: Anthony Vandenberg
Photographer: Ian Hofstetter
Stylist: Jane Collins
Food preparation: Joanne Kelly and Wendy Quisumbing
Recipes by: Kathy Knudson and members of the Murdoch Books Test Kitchen
Production: Kita George

ISBN 1 55285 886 3
ISBN 978 1 55285 886 8

Printed by Sing Cheong Printing Co. Ltd. in 2008. PRINTED IN HONG KONG.

The Publisher and stylist would like to thank Dinosaur Designs, Mud Australia, Bison Homewares and IKEA for
assistance in the photography of this book.

IMPORTANT: Those who might be at risk from the effects of salmonella poisoning (the elderly, pregnant women,
young children and those suffering from immune deficiency diseases) should consult their doctor with any
concerns about eating raw eggs.

CONVERSION GUIDE: You may find cooking times vary depending on the oven you are using. For fan-forced ovens,
as a general rule, set the oven temperature to 20°C (35°F) lower than indicated in the recipe. We have used 20 ml
(4 teaspoon) tablespoon measures. If you are using a 15 ml (3 teaspoon) tablespoon, for most recipes the difference
will not be noticeable. However, for recipes using baking powder, gelatine, bicarbonate of soda (baking soda), small
amounts of flour and cornflour (cornstarch), add an extra teaspoon for each tablespoon specified.

# EATWELLLIVEWELL

## with GROWING CHILDREN

### healthy kids' recipes and tips

Introductory text by Karen Kingham (nutritionist)

whitecap

# CONTENTS

# HEALTHY FAMILIES, HEALTHY CHILDREN

The benefits of feeding your growing children healthy food flow from childhood into adolescence and into adulthood. Good growth and development, better behaviour, concentration and learning, strong bones and teeth, a well-functioning immune system, protection from the chronic diseases of adulthood and longevity are all to be had from a balanced and nutritious diet.

The recipes in this book have been developed and tested using quality ingredients and healthy cooking methods—you'll find something for every occasion, including the all important birthday party. Not all convenience food is junk and not every meal prepared from scratch in the kitchen at home is really healthy. We've tried to achieve a healthy balance between sound nutrition and convenience, knowing that most families have busy schedules. Time-saving, healthy, commercial products have been used in many recipes or as an option to cut down preparation time.

This introductory information together with our healthy recipes will help to guide you, and your growing children, towards a healthy, happy and long life.

## Tackling health head on

Whether weight is an issue for your family or not, everyone needs to overhaul the way they eat, work and play from time to time. Unhealthy habits can easily creep up on us, taking advantage of our distraction with busy work, school and activity schedules. Often we know that our eating habits are not the best but ignore our better judgment and decide, 'just this once won't hurt'. Before you know it, these habits can become a permanent part of family routine. We may find ourselves buying takeaway rather than cooking, eating meals in front of the TV or jumping in the car rather than walking the few blocks to get the paper. Start today and get your family on a healthy eating and fitness plan.

## What to eat

Everyone, especially children, needs a variety of foods every day. Based on our needs for different nutrients, government health organizations provide recommendations about how much we should eat each day from the different food groups. This can vary with age and sex and may also differ slightly depending on what country you live in. Knowing how many serves of each food group your children need makes it easier to plan balanced and nutritious meals for the whole family.

Following is an outline of the different food groups, with recommendations for healthy eating. Some days your children might eat more, other days they will eat less. Aim for your children to be eating amounts similar to the recommendations given when they are averaged out over seven days. For more detailed information go to the websites listed on page 188.

### 1. Breads and cereals—great grain foods

Packed with carbohydrates that provide the energy children need to play, learn and grow, this food group is a good source of B vitamins, minerals and dietary fibre—especially from the wholegrain varieties. Health authorities recommend we eat less refined carbohydrates. We can do this by making half of all the grain foods we eat wholegrain and increasing foods such as brown rice, wholegrain breads, barley, burghul (bulgur), wholegrain crispbreads and crackers, rolled (porridge) oats, popcorn and wholegrain breakfast cereals.

**10 tips for a healthy family**

1. Serve wholesome, nutritious foods every day so your children learn about healthy food choices.
2. Stay away from high-fat takeaway foods. Substitute healthier versions as family treats (see pages 21–22).
3. Satisfy appetites and help prevent overeating with three meals and two to three healthy snacks each day.
4. Don't expect a clean plate. Children are good at self-regulation—they eat what they need. It is far better to waste food than let it go to their waist.
5. Make eating breakfast a rule in your house. We all do better if we eat at the beginning of the day.
6. Eat together around the table as a family (and with the TV turned off) as often as is practical—at least three nights a week.
7. Allow regular 'treats' at appropriate times and places. A child who is refused all 'treats' will covet forbidden foods and may binge on them if he or she gets the opportunity—this is not healthy.
8. Set a good example. Drink water not soft drink, eat your vegetables and don't sit in front of the TV eating crisps—unless you want your children doing these things.
9. Turn the TV and computer off—limit screen-time to one to two hours a day.
10. Enjoy an activity for an hour or more every day. Factor in going for a walk, going to the park or the beach with your children two or three times a week.

Low glycaemic index (GI) carbohydrate foods keep active children fuelled for longer, giving them more get up and go. Their slower rate of digestion and absorption makes low-GI foods more satisfying, so children are more likely to last until their next mealtime.

A diet based on low-GI carbohydrate foods is associated with a healthier body weight and lower rates of chronic adult diseases such as diabetes and heart disease. Getting children into the wholegrain and low-GI habit early is a good investment in their future.

• How much per day?

Four to six serves.

• What's a serve?

One slice of bread, ½ cup cooked rice, pasta or noodles, ½ cup cooked porridge or 1 cup ready-to-eat breakfast cereal.

## 2. Fruit and vegetables—plant power

A love of fruit and vegetables is probably the healthiest habit a child can have. It has been shown time and again that you can't replace what you get from fruit and vegetables with a vitamin or mineral supplement. Research shows that those who eat large quantities of fruit and vegetables are healthier and live longer than those who eat few or none.

Nutritionists think this has more to do with what we don't know about fruit and vegetables than about what we do know. Fruit and vegetables are packed with vitamins, minerals, fibre and energy-giving carbohydrates. But they are also rich in phytochemicals—plant chemicals that have antioxidant, anticancer or antibacterial properties. Nutritionists and scientists still have a lot to learn about phytochemicals but from what we know already the more you get from your food, the healthier you are likely to be.

Your children will get the most from this food group if you offer them varieties from these 'super groups' (listed below), which are rich in health protective phytochemicals:

- green leafy vegetables and brightly coloured vegetables and fruit: spinach, carrots, oranges, sweet potato, mango, pumpkin (winter squash), red berries, kiwi fruit, tomatoes and watermelon
- cruciferous vegetables: broccoli, cabbage, cauliflower, brussels sprouts and turnips
- the onion family: garlic, onions, leeks and chives.

While fresh is thought to be best you may be surprised to know this isn't always the case. Frozen vegetables from your freezer are not only convenient, they are nutritious. This is because frozen vegetables (and fruits) are processed and frozen soon after

### Make fruit and vegetables appealing

Many parents despair over the fact that their children don't eat enough fruit and vegetables. Try these tips to get them eating more:

- Let children pick out the fruit and vegetables when you shop.
- Involve them in meal preparation. Teach them how to wash and prepare what you need for a meal.
- Grow some at home. You don't need lots of space—a sunny spot for a pot is often all that's needed.
- Try new ways of serving. Vegetables are great crunchy and raw especially if there is something good to dip them in. Corn on the cob with fancy fork holders can be a bit different and fruit kebabs or frozen on a stick is always fun (see recipes on pages 32 and 177).
- Go for produce in season. It tastes best and is cheaper too.
- Make vegetable soup—throw in some fancy noodles and you might be surprised at how much they eat.
- Let them design their own salad with the vegetables they want—no matter if it only has one vegetable.
- Make them a fruit smoothie with fresh, frozen or tinned fruit.
- Help children 'decorate' their own home-made pizzas with a variety of colourful vegetables.

picking, which keeps many of their vitamins at their peak. Tinned fruit and vegetables also add to a healthy variety. Do take care with the amount of added sugar and salt in these products. Choose tinned fruits with no-added sugar and in natural juice and go for no-added-salt tinned vegetables whenever possible.

• How much per day?

Two serves of fruit and four to five serves of vegetables a day.

• What's a serve?

Fruit: one medium piece (banana, apple, orange, pear, peach) or two small pieces (apricots, kiwi fruit, plums), 1 cup of fruit salad or tinned fruit, 1½ tablespoons of sultanas (golden raisins), ½ cup fruit juice.

Vegetables: ½ cup cooked vegetables, 1 cup salad vegetables, one medium potato.

## 3. Dairy—the body builder

This food group provides much needed protein, fat and carbohydrates for growth, plus calcium, magnesium, phosphorus and potassium for strong teeth and bones. Iodine is also reliably found in foods of this group, especially in milk.

Nutrition experts in many countries encourage the use of lower fat dairy foods for all children from two years of age. This fosters healthy eating habits that keep weight in check and protect children from heart disease in later life, whilst continuing to provide important protein and minerals for growth.

As calcium is a nutrient some children do not get enough of, parents often worry when they refuse plain milk. As dairy is the best source of this important mineral, the daily consumption of milk is important. However, flavoured yoghurt, cheese, custard

**Low-GI energy foods for children**
Baked beans
Corn on the cob
Traditional oats
Oranges
Wholegrain English muffins
Bananas
Reduced-fat custard and
    flavoured yoghurt
Apples
Pasta
Mangoes
Basmati or Doongara rice
Reduced-fat flavoured milk

**Sugar: should you worry?**
More important than the total sugar content of a food is its complete nutritional value. A glass of chocolate milk has around the same amount of sugar as a glass of cordial, but it is far superior in the amount of body-building proteins, vitamins and minerals it contains. And a teaspoon of jam spread on wholegrain bread beats a chocolate biscuit for goodness hands down. Sugars to limit your children on are those that are empty of nutrition such as lollies, soft drinks and cordial or those that come loaded with bad fats, such as chocolate and commercial cakes and biscuits.

and even flavoured milk are all good ways for your family to get the calcium they need. In fact, U.S research shows that flavoured milk boosts calcium intake in children with little adverse effect on their weight. This may be because when children are drinking flavoured milks they aren't drinking less healthier alternatives such as soft drink or cordial.

• How much per day?

Two to three serves.

• What's a serve?

1 cup reduced-fat milk or fortified soy beverage, 1 tub (200 g) low-fat yoghurt, 2 slices low-fat cheese.

### 4. Meat and alternatives—protein power

This food group includes lean red meat, chicken, fish, eggs, legumes and nuts. It is a major source of the protein so vital for children to grow. Most children from affluent Western countries get plenty of protein. But too many unhealthy foods and drinks can mean diets fall short in protein. Vegetarian children are also at risk of not getting enough. This is because high-fibre vegetarian diets fill tummies before they have gotten all their important nutrients. Fish, eggs and dairy foods are good to include in the diets of vegetarian children for this reason.

This food group also provides hard to get minerals such as iron and zinc. Lean red meat is the richest source of iron but other members of the group still offer valuable amounts. Vegetarian protein alternatives (legumes, nuts and seeds) have a different type of iron, which is not as well absorbed as that from the other protein foods. This can be improved by including vitamin C rich foods such as citrus, broccoli, cabbage and tomatoes at the same meal.

Surveys show that many children don't get the iron they need. Enough iron is important for optimum brain development, as well as peak immune function. Iron is also essential for getting vital oxygen around the body so the muscles and body organs get enough energy. Not having enough iron leaves children tired and irritable, makes them more likely to catch colds or get sick and makes it hard for them to concentrate, making it harder to learn.

Zinc is an important nutrient for growth and repair, immunity and the sexual development that takes place at puberty. Oysters provide the richest source of this mineral but lean red meat, pork, chicken, fish, seafood and nuts also have a good amount of zinc.

• How much per day?

One to two serves a day. Aim to serve lean red meat at least three times a week and fish at least twice a week.

• What's a serve?

Two small eggs, 100 g cooked lean meat (two slices) or 80–120 g cooked fish, two small chops, ½ cup lean minced (ground) beef, tuna or salmon, ½ cup legumes (such as chickpeas, kidney beans and baked beans), 2 tablespoons of peanut butter or a small handful (30 g) of nuts.

**Vitamin D**

Not enough vitamin D makes growing bones soft, a condition known as rickets. Regular sunshine is one of the best sources of this vitamin, but even in sunny countries such as Australia, children may not get enough. To reduce the risk of developing skin cancer, 10–15 minutes of sun exposure before 10 am and after 3 pm is ideal. Walking or riding to school is one way children can get this. When days are shorter and the sun is scarce, food sources of vitamin D become more important. These include oily fish such as herring, mackerel, salmon, sardines, tuna; eggs; butter; and foods fortified with vitamin D, such as milk, margarine and breakfast cereals (check the labels to be sure).

## 5. Fats—friend or foe

This food group is an important source of energy for children. Small amounts are also essential for the absorption of the fat-soluble vitamins A, D, E and K. So while our children need some fat, they don't need a lot and the type they eat is important.

Foods with fat have a mixture of types—both healthy and unhealthy. Generally speaking we 'classify' high-fat foods by their predominant fat type; butter has mostly unhealthy saturated fats while canola and olive oil and margarines made from these have more healthy monounsaturated fats.

**Fantastic fish**

Fish is not just good for its protein, it also provides two important and often hard to get nutrients:

- Long chain omega-3 fats. These are important for growing brains and a healthy heart and blood vessels. Deep-sea fish are rich in these, but all fish and seafood have some.

- Iodine is vital for the developing brain and production of hormones and its intake is falling among children in many countries. Saltwater fish and other seafood are reliable sources of this mineral.

Too many unhealthy saturated or trans fats set our children up for future health problems, such as high cholesterol and diabetes. Healthy poly- and monounsaturated fats on the other hand can lower cholesterol, protect the heart and blood vessels and even lower the risk of certain cancers. The aim for everyone is to cut back on the unhealthy fats and swap them where possible for healthier types.

• How much per day?

This will vary from child to child depending upon their age, their weight and how active they are. Messages to lower fat intake are everywhere. But health experts agree that a greater focus on

| TYPE | WHERE YOU'LL FIND IT |
| --- | --- |
| **Healthy fats** | |
| Monounsaturated fat | olives and olive oil, avocados, peanuts and peanut oil, canola oil, macadamia nuts, hazelnuts, pecans, cashew nuts and almonds |
| Omega-6 polyunsaturated fats | sunflower, safflower, soya bean, sesame, cotton seed and grape seed oils, pine nuts and brazil nuts |
| Omega-3 polyunsaturated fats | oily types of fish (herring, sardine, mackerel, salmon and tuna), walnuts, canola oil, linseeds (flax seeds) and linseed oil, lean red meat and a range of fortified commercial foods |
| **Unhealthy fats** | |
| Saturated fats | butter, cream, palm oil, coconut milk and cream, takeaways and fried foods, fat on meat and skin on chicken, full-fat dairy foods, deli meats and most commercial cakes, pastries, confectionery and biscuits |
| Trans fats | margarines and fat spreads (some countries have less trans fats in these foods than others—check labels), deep-fried fast food, commercial cakes, pastries, pies and biscuits. Look for the words 'hydrogenated' or 'partially hydrogenated fats' on food labels. |

choosing foods with healthier fats rather than no fats is more important for health and weight. So, keep this food group in check and help your children get more of the right types of fats by:

- trimming meat
- taking the skin off chicken
- cooking with healthy oils or margarines made from these
- using reduced-fat dairy foods
- avoiding fried fast foods and commercial cakes, biscuits and snack foods
- using nuts/nut bars for snacks
- spreading avocado, peanut butter or margarine on bread instead of butter.

## Are low-fat foods making us fat?

Food manufacturers have embraced the low-fat message and supermarket aisles are loaded with products proclaiming 'fat free', 'low fat', '93% fat free' or similar. Unfortunately these products are not very helpful for controlling weight because they tend to promote a higher energy (kilojoule) intake:

1. While low-fat foods are lower in fat, especially saturated fat, some don't always have significantly fewer kilojoules. This is because extra sugars, starch or protein added to improve the flavour also bump up the kilojoules. When buying low-fat foods, compare their total kilojoules per 100 g with regular versions to make sure they are worthwhile.

2. Lower fat versions of commercial biscuits are often smaller than regular varieties. As such, people tend to eat more of them and so end up eating even more kilojoules than if they ate the regular ones.

3. Many people view low-fat foods as fat-free foods with few kilojoules and so eat more than they would of a regular fat version.

## Get up and go

For children to be fit and healthy they need to run and play—a lot. Experts recommend at least an hour or more of huff and puff type physical activity a day. Most children are naturally active and so don't need much encouragement. Indoor distractions mean it's easy for children to get side-tracked by homework, television, computer or even the mobile phone. When this happens too frequently health and weight will eventually suffer.

Of all the indoor sedentary pursuits your children do, television viewing is probably the worst. A wealth of research shows that the more TV children watch, the more likely they are to be overweight, eat a poor diet and have the risk factors that lead to health problems in adolescence and early adulthood. It's not just the fact that they expend so little energy watching TV, they are also exposed to advertising for a range of unhealthy foods, which they may pester you for later. If you plan on limiting your children's screen time you should probably be limiting yours too.

When it comes to getting off the couch and getting out, your children are most likely to take your lead—this is supported by research. Children with physically active parents are six times more likely to be active than children whose parents are sedentary. Look at your own habits and consider ways you can be more active. Daily opportunities for physical activity will steer your children towards greater health and fitness.

- Walk for transport whenever possible—to school, the corner shop, friends' houses.
- Give birthday and Christmas gifts that encourage activity such as skipping ropes, balls, bikes, bats, skates or skateboards.
- Help with basic skills development by throwing a ball or Frisbee whenever there is an opportunity.
- Hop on the bikes and try out a local cycle path.

- Be involved in community events such as clean-up campaigns or tree planting days.
- Invite friends over to play.
- Visit the beach, river or pool on hot days.
- Participate in active extracurricular activities such as gymnastics, ballet, trampolining, swimming, football or athletics.
- Make sure there are fun activities on offer as an alternative to the television or computer games.
- Organize birthday parties with active themes such as rock climbing, basketball, dancing or rollerskating/blading.
- Go on active family holidays, camp or stay by the beach and take bikes, balls and sports equipment.
- Go for a family bushwalk on the weekend.

## Family affairs

As a parent, your best chance of making a difference to your children's future health is by being a good role model. If you have unhealthy habits and are carrying too much weight or not exercising enough, the chances are your children will be too. Good eating habits are vital for healthy families leading busy lives.

## Eating as a family

Taking the time to eat together might not be possible every meal but most families can manage some regular nights each week. Children who eat regularly with their families tend to have healthier diets than those who don't—they also do better at school. Family meals also offer you the chance to practise what you teach. They provide an opportunity for a social, relaxed time with your children when they are not distracted by homework, friends on the phone, the TV or the computer. Family mealtimes can be used to plan meals ahead. Children are more likely to eat a healthy meal if they have had input into its selection and preparation.

Offer your children the same food as you are eating whenever possible—many of the recipes in this book are suitable for the whole family. Encourage them to try new foods by offering them frequently and setting a good example by eating them yourself. Enjoy more self-serve or assemble-yourself style meals such as san choy bau (page 118) and bean enchiladas (page 123). This teaches children about appropriate serve sizes and how to recognize the signs of fullness. Have they eaten enough or do they

**18**

need seconds? How full do they really feel? These are valuable lessons that can prevent the unconscious overeating that contributes to overweight and obesity.

## Eating breakfast

We all need to start the day with a good breakfast but for children it is even more important. Breakfast fuels busy brains, making them more alert, open to learning and able to concentrate on complex tasks—which in the long run means better school performance. What's more, breakfast eaters usually have healthier diets, and are far more likely to meet their recommended needs of iron, calcium, B vitamins and fibre than those who don't. Children and adults who skip breakfast are also more likely to have weight problems and are unlikely to make up nutrition shortfalls at other meals in the day.

Mornings may be a hectic time but a bowl of cereal or muesli topped with milk or yoghurt doesn't take long to prepare and eat. You can speed things up by setting the table the night before. If battles rage over sugary cereals take heed from results of research that show even these cereals make a valuable contribution to a child's daily vitamin and mineral needs. If it really bothers you, compromise and buy these cereals alternately with a healthier, higher fibre cereal of your child's choice—or try mixing the two together in a separate cereal container.

When breakfast around the kitchen table is too hard, you could whip up a breakfast smoothie (see recipes pages 50–53), consider packing them a 'breakfast' sandwich or a high-fibre muesli bar to eat on the way to school, or give them a commercial breakfast-style drink or drinking yoghurt. Remember there is always the weekend for more relaxed family breakfasts, when you can cook the healthy breakfast recipes from this book and enjoy mornings together.

## Healthy drinking

The right drinks for children are such a concern for health authorities that many countries have guidelines for healthy drinking for children. All recommend water as the best drink. Readily available, kilojoule-free and the perfect thirst quencher, children should be encouraged to drink plenty of water every day.

Reduced-fat milk is high in protein, vitamins and minerals, but has less saturated fat than whole milk. As a part of meals and snacks—plain, lightly flavoured or turned into a fruit smoothie, reduced-fat milk is a healthy and nutritious drink option.

Fruit juice has a similar amount of sugar to soft drink so should be limited to a small glass once a day. Fresh whole fruit is always a better alternative. Cordial, soft drink, flavoured mineral waters and sports drinks are also high in sugar, contain few nutrients and can lead to tooth decay and overweight.

### Snack attacks

Snacks can be a double-edged sword for both children and adults. Healthy foods eaten between meals can control appetite and prevent overeating. Research shows that healthy snacking is a strategy that can be successfully used to control weight. But, when snacking is unhealthy, it can be added to the growing list of practices to blame for weight problems.

**Healthy drinking tips**
- Always take a water bottle when you leave the house.
- Include a big jug of water on the table at mealtimes.
- Make water drinking fun using ice cubes, fruit slices and 'crazy' drinking straws.
- Invest in a water filter jug for the fridge if your water doesn't taste that great.
- Dilute cordial with more water than recommended.
- Keep fizzy drinks for special occasions and serve them up in small glasses.
- Make milkshakes and smoothies as nutritious and filling snacks.

Children need to snack because their small tummies can't fit in enough to last until their next main meal, so snacks make a substantial contribution to children's nutrition needs. Studies estimate snacks make up as much as half of a child's daily energy intake, which is why it is important that snacks aren't just empty kilojoules and offer a healthy range of vitamins and minerals.

Healthy snacks for children can be based on the same foods as meals. Think of them as a mini-meal. If keeping your children away from unhealthy snacks at home proves to be a problem, take them off your shopping list and out of the pantry. Alternatively, negotiate limits for occasional snacks such as cakes, doughnuts, chocolates, sweets, savoury and sweet biscuits, and crisps.

These snack suggestions will keep up energy levels:
- Tub of low-fat flavoured yoghurt or drinking yoghurt
- Wholegrain crackers or crispbread and low-fat cheese
- Rice crackers or corn cakes and salsa dip
- Scones or pikelets
- Snack-sized tin of baked beans

- Dried fruit and nut mix
- Mug of soup and slice of wholegrain bread toast
- Fresh fruit salad
- Reduced-fat milkshake or fruit smoothie
- Fruit snack pack
- Air-popped popcorn
- Raisin toast
- Corn on the cob

## Eating out and takeaways

What do you do when you are too tired to cook and want an easy takeaway or meal out? These times don't have to be the exception to healthy family rules, especially when you know the tricks and traps for the unwary.

Although fast-food chains are probably the most attractive option for your children, your local restaurant offers the best chance of a healthy meal for your family. If you find you can't resist the pestering for a cute toy your children have seen on television, the good news is that fast-food franchises are introducing healthier menus and the use of healthier fats.

There are still traps to avoid when visiting the fast-food restaurant. Avoiding the meal deals and super sizing, and saying no to extra fries will go a long way to keeping fat and kilojoules down in your family's fast-food meal.

Maintain your family's healthy eating efforts with these tips for healthy choices.

- Fast food: smaller or home-style burgers with plenty of salad, thin crust small pizzas, grilled chicken or fish
- Italian: risotto or pasta (plain or filled) with tomato-based sauces, marinara, minestrone, gelato
- Indian: tandoori, curries with yoghurt-based sauces, vegetable curries, steamed rice, chapattis, dhal, raita
- Chinese: steamed rice, clear soup, won ton soup, braised or stir-fried dishes, green or jasmine tea
- Mexican: fajitas, salads, burritos or soft flour tortillas with lean meat, chicken or pinto beans, fresh salsa
- Thai: hot and sour soups, salads, stir-fried meat, seafood and vegetables, steamed rice.

## Growing up—not out

International obesity organizations estimate one in every ten children is overweight or obese. In countries such as America, Australia, the United Kingdom and Europe this may be even higher, closer to one in three or four. The health consequences of this obesity epidemic for our children are serious. Statistics like these are overwhelming. But as a parent you can do something to prevent your children becoming overweight—reading this book is a good start.

**'Takeaway' food at home**
Children love the 'extras' that go with takeaway. Entice them with your own version of fast food by wrapping fish and chunky wedges (page 117) in newspaper, popping Thai chicken burgers (page 129) into a paper bag or serving hokkien noodle and beef stir-fry (page 124) in cardboard noodle boxes.

## Why overweight is unhealthy

Carrying an unhealthy amount of weight can lead to serious health problems for children, some of which you wouldn't expect to see in childhood or adolescence, but which are becoming increasingly more common. These include:

- High blood pressure
- High blood cholesterol
- Type 2 diabetes
- Sleep apnoea
- Fatty liver
- Foot and knee problems
- Social and psychological problems

## How we get fat

Two main factors determine whether we become overweight or not; our genes and our environment. Look to yourself and your own parents to see your child's genetic destiny. Your child's body weight, shape, size and height are all genetically determined. If your family has a history of weight problems, it's likely your children will too. If your weight is at an unhealthy level your children are ten times more likely to have weight problems according to the research.

Over the past decade or more our environment has been playing a greater role than our genes. Environmental influences on weight include what we eat and how much exercise or physical activity we get. More fast, highly processed foods, cheap and convenient snacks, portion distortion and lots of messages to eat, eat, eat, mean many children are getting too much of the wrong foods.

A number of factors conspire against children getting the exercise they need. We fear for their safety when playing in the street and over-full schedules don't allow time to walk children to school, play at friends' houses or go to the park. TV and computers also make sitting around more attractive to some children than running around outside.

Combine overeating poor quality foods with not enough physical activity and you have the perfect environment for raising children with more than just puppy fat. Getting the energy balance right so that the energy your children get from food matches the energy they expend in physical activity will protect them against unhealthy weight gains.

### Weighing in—parents

To find out if you need to worry about your children's weight first take a look at yourself. Could you lose weight? Has your waist been creeping outward over the past few years? Body Mass Index (BMI) is a way of working out body fatness. Carefully measure your height in metres and weight in kilograms and apply it to the BMI equation below.

BMI = weight (kilograms) ÷ height (metres) squared

For example: if your weight is 68 kg and you are 165 cm (1.65 m) tall, then the calculation is:

68 ÷ (1.65 x 1.65) = 25

Provided you are over 20 years of age you can use your BMI to work out how healthy your weight is:

below 18.5 means you are underweight;

between 18.5 and 25 means you are a healthy weight;

greater than 25 means you are overweight;

greater than 30 means you are obese.

If your BMI reveals the kilos have been creeping on, take action to stop the spread—it will have positive benefits for everyone in your family not just you.

Note: To use imperial measurements use the following equation: BMI = weight (in pounds) ÷ height (in inches) squared x 703.

## Weighing in—children

Now take a look at your children. For children and teenagers between two and 20 years, body fatness is determined in much the same way as adults—you need to know how tall they are and how much they weigh—BUT because young people are still growing, their BMI can't be compared to a fixed range in the same way adults BMI can.

Children's BMIs change as they grow. As they get taller, heavier and older their body fatness changes. For this

reason it is a good idea to measure BMI on a regular basis in the same way you checked their growth when they were babies, but not as often. At each birthday and perhaps once in between is enough. A series of BMI measurements over time enables you to compare how they are doing by marking their position on a body mass index-for-age percentile chart such as the one on page 26. Charts such as these will show you how healthy your child's weight is. To use the chart look for your child's age on the boys' or girls' chart. Mark the spot at the point their age intersects with their calculated BMI, which you have worked out in the same way you did your own. Are your children overweight, a healthy weight or underweight?

Children with a BMI between the 5th and the 85th percentile (green shaded area) are at a healthy weight for their height. Children in this healthy BMI range are least likely to have health problems.

If your child's BMI is not in the healthy weight range but is:

- Less than the 5th percentile (blue shaded area) then they could be underweight
- Over the 85th percentile (yellow shaded area) but under the 95th percentile your child could be overweight
- Greater than the 95th percentile (red shaded area) and they are likely to be obese.

**25**

### Body Mass Index-for-age Boys 5 to 13 years

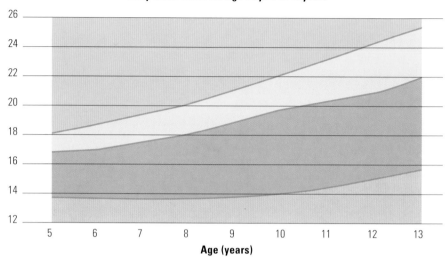

Age (years)

### Body Mass Index-for-age Girls 5 to 13 years

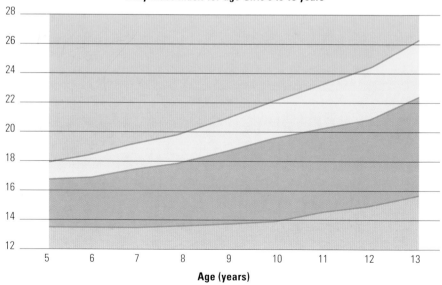

Age (years)

The above charts were adapted from those developed by the National Centre for Health Statistics in collaboration with the National Centre for Chronic Disease Prevention and Health Promotion (2000) www.cdc.gov/growthcharts/

## When it's not puppy fat

If your child's BMI is in the yellow or red shaded areas, then your child is probably carrying unhealthy levels of fat. Overweight or obese children don't just have puppy fat and won't grow out of their excess weight without help.

The good news is that while it can be a long, slow process for adults, weight control in children is easier. With growth on their side the aim for most children is not to lose weight, but to keep it steady for a while. Holding weight constant allows growth to do the work. The taller they become while maintaining the same weight, the less fat they have, the lower their BMI gets and the healthier they are. This is known as 'growing into your weight'.

### Healthy weight goals for all the family

- Eat two pieces of any type of fresh fruit every day.
- Enjoy two to three serves of low-fat dairy each day.
- Spend 30 minutes each day riding a bike/kicking a ball/bouncing on the trampoline or enjoying some other physical activity.
- Encourage children to plan a healthy meal of their own choice each week. Help them make a shopping list and buy the ingredients together.

## Involve everyone in the family

In the beginning seeking help is a good idea. A dietitian will help you identify the most important changes your family needs to make and guide you in setting realistic goals. Avoid weight-based goals or those focused on deprivation.

Any efforts at managing children's weight will be more effective if the whole family is involved. This book will also be a valuable resource. Recipes have been selected to have less fat and sugar. Where possible, there are tips on lowering kilojoules further using alternative ingredients or cooking methods. And many of the meals you prepare from this book can be enjoyed by the entire family, not just your children. A healthy home works towards improving the eating and exercising habits of everyone in the family, not just the one with the 'weight problem'.

**Disclaimer:** This book provides general information about healthy eating habits essential for growing children aged five to twelve years, as well as recipes suited to this age group. Note that the nutritional analysis of recipes does not include serving suggestions or garnishes. The advice given in this book may not be sufficient for children with specific dietary needs. Neither the author nor the publisher can be held responsible for claims arising from the inappropriate use or incorrect interpretation of any of the dietary advice described in this book.

# BREAKFAST

# HOME-MADE MUESLI

ALTHOUGH MANY COMMERCIAL BREAKFAST CEREALS CAN BE USED FOR YOUR CHILD'S BREAKFAST, SOME ARE HIGH IN SUGAR AND SALT. THIS MUESLI HAS ALL THE GOODNESS OF WHOLE GRAINS AND DRIED FRUITS, WITHOUT ANY UNWANTED EXTRAS, AND IS A GREAT WAY TO START THE DAY.

**150 g (5½ oz/1½ cups) wholegrain rolled (porridge) oats**
**2 tbsp wheat germ**
**25 g (1 oz/⅓ cup) unprocessed wheat bran**
**60 g (2¼ oz/½ cup) sultanas (golden raisins)**
**30 g (1 oz/⅓ cup) dried apple, chopped**

**90 g (3¼ oz/½ cup) dried apricots, chopped**

PREP TIME: 10 MINUTES
COOKING TIME: NIL
SERVES 6

Combine all the ingredients together and store in an airtight container until needed (it will keep for up to 4 weeks).

Serve with cold or warm reduced-fat milk. If desired, top with other dried fruits, fresh fruit, yoghurt or a drizzle of honey.

nutrition per serve: Energy 796 kJ (190 Cal); Fat 2.5 g; Saturated fat 0.4 g; Protein 4.8 g; Carbohydrate 34.2 g; Fibre 6.2 g; Cholesterol 0 mg

# BANANA PORRIDGE

A WHOLEGRAIN CEREAL SUCH AS OATS IS RICH IN ENERGY-GIVING CARBOHYDRATE, FIBRE AND MINERALS. TEAM THE OATS WITH BANANA AND IT BECOMES A GREAT SOURCE OF B VITAMINS, INCLUDING FOLATE, AS WELL AS VITAMIN C AND POTASSIUM.

**50 g (1¾ oz/½ cup) wholegrain rolled (porridge) oats**
**375 ml (13 fl oz/1½ cups) reduced-fat milk**
**1 banana, sliced**
**2 tsp soft brown sugar**

PREP TIME: 5 MINUTES
COOKING TIME: 5 MINUTES
SERVES 2

Put the oats and 125 ml (4 fl oz/½ cup) of the milk in a small saucepan over medium heat and stir to combine. Add the remaining milk and bring to the boil, stirring constantly. Add half the banana, then reduce the heat to low and simmer, stirring occasionally, for 3–4 minutes, or until the oats are thick and creamy.

Divide the porridge between two bowls and mix with a little extra milk to cool the porridge a little. Top with the remaining sliced banana and sprinkle with the sugar.

HINT:
• If preferred, use water instead of milk to make the porridge (or use half milk and half water).

nutrition per serve: Energy 1035 kJ (247 Cal); Fat 4.9 g; Saturated fat 2.1 g; Protein 11.1 g; Carbohydrate 38.9 g; Fibre 2.8 g; Cholesterol 14 mg

# FRUIT KEBABS WITH HONEYED YOGHURT

**4 strawberries, hulled and cut in half**

**1 mango, cut into large dice**

**1 banana, cut into chunks**

**1 apple, unpeeled, cut into large dice**

**4 tbsp low-fat vanilla yoghurt**

**2 tsp honey**

**1 tbsp flaked almonds, toasted**

PREP TIME: 10 MINUTES

COOKING TIME: NIL

MAKES 6

You will need six 15 cm (6 in) wooden skewers. Thread five pieces of fruit onto each skewer, alternating the fruit along the skewers.

Combine the yoghurt and honey in a small bowl. Place two or three fruit skewers on each serving plate, drizzle with the honeyed yoghurt and sprinkle with the toasted almonds.

FRUIT ALWAYS MAKES A GREAT SUMMER BREAKFAST AND IS A RICH SOURCE OF HEALTHY ANTIOXIDANTS. YOU CAN MAKE THESE KEBABS WITH YOUR CHILD'S FAVOURITE FRUIT BUT IT'S ALSO A GOOD CHANCE TO SLIP IN ONE OR TWO 'NEW' FRUITS, SUCH AS FRESH LYCHEES OR PINEAPPLE.

nutrition per fruit kebab: Energy 350 kJ (84 Cal)
Fat 1.3 g
Saturated fat 0.1 g
Protein 2.1 g
Carbohydrate 15 g
Fibre 1.8 g
Cholesterol 1 mg

# LAYERED CEREAL AND APPLE YOGHURT

EATING A HEALTHY BREAKFAST WILL GIVE YOUR CHILD MORE ENERGY AND WILL HELP MAINTAIN THEIR CONCENTRATION LEVELS THROUGHOUT THE MORNING. THIS RECIPE IS A GREAT ONE FOR QUICK STARTS, AS NO COOKING IS NEEDED.

**125 g (4½ oz/½ cup) low-fat plain or fruit-flavoured yoghurt**
**½ red apple, unpeeled, finely grated**
**70 g (2½ oz/1 cup) crunchy breakfast cereal, such as Sultana Bran Crunch™**
**½ tsp soft brown sugar or honey**

PREP TIME: 10 MINUTES
COOKING TIME: NIL
SERVES 2

Combine the yoghurt and apple in a small bowl. Layer the cereal and yoghurt mixture in small, wide glasses and sprinkle the top with brown sugar or honey. Serve immediately.

HINTS:
• You can use any type of cereal for this breakfast, such as natural muesli, but choose one that won't go soft too quickly when mixed with the yoghurt.
• Add some oat bran or sunflower seeds to the cereal for added fibre.

nutrition per serve: Energy 780 kJ (186 Cal); Fat 0.7 g; Saturated fat 0.2 g; Protein 6.2 g; Carbohydrate 36.4 g; Fibre 3.7 g; Cholesterol 3 mg

# HOME-MADE BAKED BEANS

BAKED BEANS MAKE A HEARTY, NOURISHING BREAKFAST—A GREAT START
TO A COLD WINTER'S DAY. THIS MEAL PROVIDES A HEALTHY DOSE OF FIBRE,
AS WELL AS VITAMINS, PROTEIN AND ANTIOXIDANTS. THIS IS A LOW-GI MEAL
THE WHOLE FAMILY WILL ENJOY.

**2 bacon slices, rind removed, chopped**
**2 x 400 g (14 oz) tins cannellini beans,**
   **drained and rinsed**
**400 g (14 oz) tin no-added-salt diced**
   **tomatoes**
**125 ml (4 fl oz/½ cup) reduced-salt**
   **vegetable stock**
**1 bay leaf**
**2 tbsp chopped flat-leaf (Italian) parsley**

**pinch of dried thyme**
**2 tsp olive oil**
**30 g (1 oz/¼ cup) low-fat grated**
   **cheddar cheese**

PREP TIME: 10 MINUTES
COOKING TIME: 45 MINUTES
SERVES 4

Preheat the oven to 180°C (350°F/Gas 4).

Put the bacon in a small frying pan over medium heat and fry for 2–3 minutes, or until just cooked and starting to brown.

Put the beans in a casserole dish and add the bacon, tomato, stock, bay leaf, parsley, thyme and oil. Season with freshly ground black pepper. Bake, covered, for 40 minutes.

Serve the beans with wholegrain toast or muffins and sprinkle with the cheese.

HINTS:
• If you want a thicker sauce, remove the lid of the casserole dish and cook for a further 10 minutes, or until reduced to the desired consistency.
• Use low-fat bacon slices to lower the fat content of this dish further.

nutrition per serve: Energy 867 kJ (207 Cal); Fat 7.4 g; Saturated fat 2.3 g; Protein 12.8 g; Carbohydrate 21.6 g; Fibre 9.3 g; Cholesterol 12 mg

RESEARCH SHOWS THAT A
HEALTHY DIET IS ENCOURAGED
WHEN CHILDREN REGULARLY
EAT WITH THEIR FAMILY. ENJOY
THIS BREAKFAST ON WEEKENDS,
WHEN THE FAMILY HAS TIME TO
SIT DOWN AND EAT TOGETHER.

nutrition per serve: Energy 1007 kJ (241 Cal)

Fat 11.3 g

Saturated fat 2.5 g

Protein 11.7 g

Carbohydrate 21 g

Fibre 3.7 g

Cholesterol 187 mg

# BAKED EGGS

**3 tomatoes (about 300 g/10½ oz)**
**2 tsp olive oil**
**1 garlic clove, crushed**
**4 eggs**
**2 tbsp snipped chives**
**4 thick slices wholegrain bread**
**15 g (½ oz) margarine**

PREP TIME: 15 MINUTES
COOKING TIME: 30 MINUTES
SERVES 4

To make the tomato sauce, score a cross in the base of each tomato, place in a heatproof bowl and cover with boiling water. Leave for 1 minute, or until the skins start to come away. Drain, plunge into a bowl of iced water, then peel away the skin. Cut in half and scoop out the seeds with a teaspoon, then roughly chop the flesh.

Heat the oil in a heavy-based frying pan. Add the garlic and cook for 30 seconds, then add the tomato and season with a little freshly ground black pepper. Cook over medium heat for 15 minutes, or until the sauce has thickened. Set aside.

Preheat the oven to 180°C (350°F/Gas 4).

Lightly grease four 125 ml (4 fl oz/½ cup) ramekins, then carefully break 1 egg into each, trying not to break the yolk. Pour the tomato sauce evenly around the outside of each egg, so the yolk is still visible. Sprinkle with the chives and cover with a piece of foil. Place the ramekins in a deep baking dish and pour in enough hot water to come halfway up the sides of the ramekins. Bake for about 15 minutes, or until the egg white is set, removing the foil halfway through cooking time.

Toast the bread and lightly spread the slices with the margarine, then cut into thick fingers. Serve immediately with the cooked eggs.

HINTS:
• If you are short on time, use bottled tomato passata (puréed tomatoes) instead of making the tomato sauce.
• Use omega-3-enriched eggs to add more healthy essential fatty acids to this meal.

# RICOTTA CRUMPETS WITH PEAR

SCHOOL-DAY MORNINGS CAN BE A PARTICULARLY HECTIC TIME. THIS NUTRITIOUS BREAKFAST CAN BE COOKED AND ON THE TABLE IN UNDER 10 MINUTES. FOR ADDED FIBRE, LEAVE THE PEAR UNPEELED AND USE WHOLEMEAL CRUMPETS.

**2 crumpets**
**2 tbsp ricotta cheese**
**1 pear, peeled, thinly sliced**
**2 tsp honey or maple syrup**
**1 tbsp sultanas (golden raisins)**
**pinch of ground cinnamon (optional)**

PREP TIME: 5 MINUTES
COOKING TIME: 5 MINUTES
SERVES 1–2

Toast the crumpets and while still warm, spread with the ricotta cheese.

Top the crumpets with slices of the pear, drizzle with the honey and sprinkle with the sultanas and ground cinnamon if desired.

HINTS:
• Swapping regular ricotta cheese for low fat will cut the fat further in this recipe.
• Children with small appetites may need only one crumpet each, but for active or older children with larger appetites two or more crumpets may be necessary.

nutrition per serve (2): Energy 872 kJ (208 Cal); Fat 2.8 g; Saturated fat 1.5 g; Protein 5 g; Carbohydrate 40 g; Fibre 3.1 g; Cholesterol 10 mg

# BREAKFAST FRUIT COMPOTE

THIS FRUITY BREAKFAST IS FULL OF FLAVOUR AND IS A GREAT SOURCE OF FIBRE, CALCIUM AND POTASSIUM, WITH SMALL BUT IMPORTANT AMOUNTS OF IRON AND BETA-CAROTENE. SERVE THE COMPOTE WITH HOME-MADE MUESLI, PORRIDGE OR BREAKFAST CEREAL.

**50 g (1¾ oz/⅓ cup) dried apricots, quartered**
**50 g (1¾ oz/¼ cup) pitted prunes, quartered**
**50 g (1¾ oz/⅔ cup) dried pears, chopped**
**50 g (1¾ oz/⅔ cup) dried peaches, chopped**
**185 ml (6 fl oz/¾ cup) orange juice**

**1 cinnamon stick**
**4 tbsp low-fat plain yoghurt**

PREP TIME: 5 MINUTES
COOKING TIME: 10 MINUTES
SERVES 4

Put the dried fruit, orange juice and cinnamon stick in a saucepan and stir to combine. Bring to the boil, then reduce the heat to low, cover and simmer for 10 minutes, or until the fruit is plump and softened. Discard the cinnamon stick.

Serve the compote with your choice of muesli, porridge or cereal, drizzled with the cooking liquid and topped with a dollop of the yoghurt.

HINT:
• Store the compote in an airtight container in the refrigerator for up to 1 week.

nutrition per serve: Energy 573 kJ (137 Cal); Fat 0.3 g; Saturated fat 0.02 g; Protein 3.1 g; Carbohydrate 28.4 g; Fibre 4.6 g; Cholesterol 1 mg

# FRENCH TOAST

**1 egg, lightly beaten**
**2 tsp reduced-fat milk**
**margarine or oil, for frying**
**2 thick slices wholemeal (whole-wheat)**
**bread (see Hint)**
**4 strawberries, sliced**
**2 tsp honey or maple syrup**

PREP TIME: 5 MINUTES
COOKING TIME: 2 MINUTES
SERVES 1–2

Combine the egg and milk in a bowl large enough to fit the bread, and beat lightly with a fork.

Heat the margarine or oil in a frying pan over medium heat. Dip the bread into the egg mixture, drain off the excess, then cook until golden brown on both sides. Remove to a plate, top with the strawberries and drizzle with honey or maple syrup.

HINT:
• If desired, cut the bread into different shapes using biscuit cutters; however, you will need to increase the bread to four slices to allow for wastage.

BREAD IS AN IMPORTANT STAPLE
FOOD FOR GROWING CHILDREN.
VARY THE TYPES OF BREAD FOR
THIS RECIPE BY USING RYE,
WHOLEGRAIN OR EVEN FRUIT
BREAD. THIS IS A DELICIOUS
BREAKFAST FOR A WEEKEND TREAT.

nutrition per serve (2): Energy 725 kJ (173 Cal)

Fat 5.5 g

Saturated fat 1.3 g

Protein 7.7 g

Carbohydrate 22 g

Fibre 3 g

Cholesterol 94 mg

# SCRAMBLED EGGS WITH SWEET CORN

THE COMBINATION OF EGGS WITH THEIR HIGH QUALITY PROTEIN, AND CORN, A GOOD SOURCE OF LOW-GI CARBOHYDRATE AND FIBRE, MAKES THIS MEAL A NUTRITIOUS AND SUSTAINING START TO YOUR CHILD'S DAY.

**2 x 125 g (4½ oz) tins creamed corn**
**15 g (½ oz) margarine**
**2½ tsp cornflour (cornstarch)**
**250 ml (9 fl oz/1 cup) reduced-fat milk**
**6 eggs**
**1 tbsp reduced-fat milk, extra**
**1–2 tsp margarine, extra**

PREP TIME: 10 MINUTES
COOKING TIME: 10 MINUTES
SERVES 4

Put the corn and margarine in a saucepan. Combine the cornflour and 1 tablespoon of the milk in a bowl and stir until smooth, then add the remaining milk, stirring well. Pour into the saucepan with the corn and bring to the boil. Simmer, stirring, for 2–3 minutes, or until the sauce thickens. Keep warm.

Beat the eggs and extra milk together and season with freshly ground black pepper. Melt the extra margarine in a frying pan over low heat and pour in the egg mixture. Cook gently, stirring occasionally, for 2–3 minutes, or until just firm. Transfer to a plate and pour on the sweet corn sauce. Serve with wholegrain toast or English muffins.

HINT:
• Lower the fat in this recipe by using a non-stick frying pan or cooking oil spray.

nutrition per serve: Energy 985 kJ (235 Cal); Fat 12.9 g; Saturated fat 3.7 g; Protein 13.6 g; Carbohydrate 15.7 g; Fibre 2.1 g; Cholesterol 286 mg

# MUSHROOMS WITH SOURDOUGH

THIS DISH IS A RICH SOURCE OF FOLATE AND FIBRE, AND PROVIDES GOOD AMOUNTS OF ANTIOXIDANTS AND NIACIN. MUSHROOMS MAKE A FLAVOURSOME BREAKFAST THAT CAN BE ENJOYED BY THE WHOLE FAMILY.

**MUSHROOM SAUCE**

1 tbsp olive oil

800 g (1 lb 12 oz/8 cups) mixed mushrooms (flat, button, open-cap), chopped

2 garlic cloves, crushed

1 tsp finely chopped thyme

125 ml (4 fl oz/½ cup) reduced-salt vegetable stock

1 large handful parsley, finely chopped

4 thick slices sourdough or wholemeal (whole-wheat) bread

baby English spinach, to serve (optional)

shaved parmesan cheese, to serve (optional)

PREP TIME: 10 MINUTES

COOKING TIME: 20 MINUTES

SERVES 4

To make the mushroom sauce, heat the oil in a large frying pan, add the mushrooms and cook over high heat for 4–5 minutes, or until soft. Add the garlic and thyme, season with freshly ground black pepper and cook for 2–3 minutes. Add 185 ml (6 fl oz/¾ cup) water and cook until the water has evaporated. Add the stock, then reduce the heat and cook for a further 3–4 minutes, or until the stock has reduced and thickened. Stir in the parsley.

Grill (broil) or toast the bread until golden on both sides. Divide among the serving plates and top with the mushrooms. Top with spinach and parmesan shavings if desired.

nutrition per serve: Energy 831 kJ (199 Cal); Fat 6.2 g; Saturated fat 0.8 g; Protein 10.5 g; Carbohydrate 20.8 g; Fibre 8.9 g; Cholesterol 0 mg

A SOURCE OF VITAMIN C AND OTHER ANTIOXIDANTS, BLUEBERRIES MAKE THESE PANCAKES A NUTRITIOUS BREAKFAST CHOICE. THE COULIS CAN ALSO BE STIRRED THROUGH YOGHURT OR DRIZZLED OVER FRUIT SALAD, PORRIDGE OR MUESLI.

nutrition per pancake: Energy 1206 kJ (288 Cal)
Fat 7.5 g
Saturated fat 1.8 g
Protein 7.7 g
Carbohydrate 46.4 g
Fibre 2.6 g
Cholesterol 50 mg

# BLUEBERRY PANCAKES WITH COULIS

**BLUEBERRY COULIS**
**310 g (11 oz/2 cups) fresh or frozen blueberries**
**2 tsp icing (confectioners') sugar**

**250 g (9 oz/2 cups) plain (all-purpose) flour**
**2 tsp baking powder**
**1 tsp bicarbonate of soda (baking soda)**
**90 g (3¼ oz/⅓ cup) sugar**
**2 eggs**

**60 g (2¼ oz) margarine, melted**
**310 ml (10¾ fl oz/1¼ cups) reduced-fat milk**
**310 g (11 oz/2 cups) fresh or frozen blueberries**
**4 tbsp low-fat plain yoghurt, to serve**

PREP TIME: 20 MINUTES
COOKING TIME: 20 MINUTES
MAKES 8

To make the blueberry coulis, put the blueberries in a blender or food processor and blend until puréed. Strain the coulis through a fine sieve to remove the skin and to make a smooth sauce. Stir in the icing sugar. Set aside until needed.

Sift the flour, baking powder and bicarbonate of soda into a large bowl. Add the sugar and make a well in the centre. Using a fork, whisk the eggs, melted margarine and milk together in a bowl and add to the dry ingredients, stirring just to combine (add more milk if you prefer a thinner batter). Gently fold in the blueberries.

Heat a non-stick frying pan over low heat and brush lightly with melted margarine or oil. Pour 125 ml (4 fl oz/½ cup) of the batter into the pan and spread out to make a pancake about 15 cm (6 in) in diameter. Cook for about 3 minutes, or until bubbles appear and pop on the surface, then turn the pancake over and cook the other side (these pancakes can be difficult to handle, so take care when turning). Transfer to a plate and cover with a tea towel (dish towel) to keep warm while you cook the remaining batter.

Serve the blueberry pancakes topped with a dollop of yoghurt and drizzled with the blueberry coulis.

HINTS:
• If you use frozen blueberries, there is no need to thaw them first.
• Store any leftover blueberry coulis in the refrigerator for up to 3 days.

# BANANA PANCAKES

A HIGHLY NUTRITIOUS FRUIT, BANANAS CONTAIN FIBRE, POTASSIUM AND THE VITAMINS C AND B6. THEY ARE ALSO A SOURCE OF CARBOHYDRATES TO FUEL YOUR CHILD'S MORNING AND SEE THEM THROUGH TO THEIR NEXT MEAL OR SNACK.

**2 very ripe bananas, mashed**
**150 g (5½ oz/1 cup) wholemeal**
  **(whole-wheat) flour**
**2 tsp baking powder**
**½ tsp ground cinnamon**
**pinch of ground nutmeg**
**250 ml (9 fl oz/1 cup) reduced-fat milk**
**1 tbsp maple syrup or honey**

**maple syrup or honey, extra, to serve**
**sliced banana, to serve (optional)**

PREP TIME: 20 MINUTES + 1 HOUR STANDING
COOKING TIME: 25 MINUTES
MAKES 10

Put the mashed banana in a large bowl. Sift the flour, baking powder, cinnamon and nutmeg onto the banana and return the husks left in the sieve to the bowl. Stir until the flour is moistened but not totally combined with the mashed banana.

Make a well in the centre, add the milk and maple syrup and stir constantly until smooth. Set aside for 1 hour.

Heat a large non-stick frying pan over medium heat and brush lightly with oil or melted margarine. Cook the pancakes in batches, using about 60 ml (2 fl oz/¼ cup) of batter for each pancake. Cook for 3–4 minutes, or until small bubbles appear on the surface. Then, using a spatula, gently turn the pancakes over, loosening the edges first so they don't stick to the pan, and cook for another 3 minutes. Remove from the pan and keep warm. Repeat with the remaining batter.

Serve drizzled with extra maple syrup and a few slices of banana if desired.

nutrition per pancake: Energy 381 kJ (91 Cal); Fat 0.7 g; Saturated fat 0.3 g; Protein 3.2 g; Carbohydrate 16.9 g; Fibre 2.2 g; Cholesterol 2 mg

# FLUFFY OMELETTE

THE ULTIMATE IN CONVENIENCE FOOD, EGGS MAKE A PERFECT MEAL
AT ANY TIME OF THE DAY FOR A GROWING CHILD—DON'T JUST SAVE
THEM FOR BREAKFAST.

**2 egg yolks**
**4 egg whites**
**2 tsp margarine**

PREP TIME: 5 MINUTES
COOKING TIME: 10 MINUTES
SERVES 2

Lightly beat the egg yolks with 2 teaspoons water. Beat the egg whites in a clean, dry bowl until soft peaks form, then stir in the yolk mixture.

Melt half the margarine in a small frying pan and pour in half the egg mixture. Cook quickly on one side, then turn and cook until just firm. Repeat with the remaining egg mixture. Serve with wholegrain toast and slices of tomato if desired.

VARIATIONS:
• Flaked red salmon, finely chopped sautéed zucchini (courgette) and onion, mushrooms, tomato or grated cheddar cheese can be used to fill the omelette. Place the filling along the centre of the omelette on the uncooked side, then fold over to enclose the filling. Cook until the omelette is cooked through, turning once.

nutrition per serve: Energy 469 kJ (112 Cal); Fat 8.1 g; Saturated fat 2.1 g; Protein 9.6 g; Carbohydrate 0.3 g; Fibre 0 g; Cholesterol 178 mg

# POTATO RÖSTI WITH BACON

20 g (¾ oz) margarine
1 onion, grated
1 garlic clove, crushed
2 bacon slices, finely chopped
600 g (1 lb 5 oz) all-purpose potatoes, such
   as desiree, peeled and coarsely grated
1–2 tbsp finely chopped sage or flat-leaf
   (Italian) parsley
canola or olive oil spray

PREP TIME: 15 MINUTES
COOKING TIME: 20 MINUTES
MAKES 12

Melt the margarine in a large frying pan. Add the onion, garlic and bacon and cook over medium heat, stirring, for about 5 minutes, or until soft. Add the grated potato and cook, stirring, for 1–2 minutes, or until the mixture is sticky.

Remove from the heat and stir in the sage and season with a little salt and pepper. Mix well, then spread onto a flat tray and leave until cool enough to handle.

Heat a heavy-based frying pan or barbecue grill plate over high heat. Divide the potato mixture into 12 portions and shape each portion into even-sized patties. Spray the pan with a little oil, add the patties in batches and cook for 3–5 minutes on each side, or until golden brown and crisp, using a spatula to press each rösti to a 5 cm (2 in) round, taking care not to loosen the mixture. Drain on crumpled paper towels and serve hot.

REFRIGERATING LEFTOVERS
OVERNIGHT WILL LOWER THE GI
OF THESE POTATO RÖSTI, MAKING
THEM A GREAT SCHOOL LUNCHBOX
ADDITION THAT WILL EASILY KEEP
THEM GOING UNTIL HOME TIME.

nutrition per rösti: Energy 247 kJ (59 Cal)
Fat 2.3 g
Saturated fat 0.5 g
Protein 2.7 g
Carbohydrate 6.2 g
Fibre 0.9 g
Cholesterol 4 mg

# ICED BANANA SMOOTHIE

THIS SMOOTHIE MAKES A QUICK AND REFRESHING SUMMER DRINK FOR BREAKFAST AND IS GREAT FOR CHILDREN WHO DON'T HAVE MUCH OF AN APPETITE IN THE MORNING. KEEP A FEW FROZEN BANANAS IN THE FREEZER, SO YOU'LL ALWAYS HAVE SOME ON STANDBY.

**1 large banana, cut into chunks and frozen**
**250 ml (9 fl oz/1 cup) reduced-fat milk**
**60 g (2¼ oz/¼ cup) low-fat vanilla yoghurt**
**1 tsp wheat germ**
**1 tsp honey (optional)**

PREP TIME: 5 MINUTES
COOKING TIME: NIL
SERVES 2

Put the banana, milk, yoghurt and wheat germ in a blender and process until smooth and thick. Sweeten with a little honey if preferred. Serve immediately in two glasses.

VARIATIONS:
• Instead of bananas and vanilla yoghurt, use frozen peach or mango slices with peach or mango-flavoured yoghurt.

nutrition per serve: Energy 629 kJ (150 Cal); Fat 2 g; Saturated fat 1.2 g; Protein 8.1 g; Carbohydrate 24.4 g; Fibre 1.5 g; Cholesterol 11 mg

# SUMMER FRUIT SOY SMOOTHIE

THIS SOY BREAKFAST SMOOTHIE MAKES A GREAT DAIRY-FREE BREAKFAST ALTERNATIVE. TRY SUBSTITUTING TINNED PEACH HALVES WHEN FRESH ARE UNAVAILABLE. AND, BECAUSE OF THEIR CONCENTRATED FLAVOUR YOU ONLY NEED HALF AS MANY.

**1 banana**

**4 peaches, peeled and chopped**

**175 g (6 oz/¾ cup) apricot and mango soy yoghurt or vanilla soy yoghurt**

**1 tbsp wheat germ or oat bran**

**1 tsp natural vanilla extract**

**625 ml (21½ fl oz/2½ cups) plain soy milk or vanilla soy milk**

**1 tbsp maple syrup or honey (optional)**

**ice cubes, to serve**

**peach slices, extra, to serve**

PREP TIME: 10 MINUTES

COOKING TIME: NIL

SERVES 4

Put the banana, peaches, yoghurt, wheat germ, vanilla and 250 ml (9 fl oz/1 cup) of the soy milk in a blender. Blend for 30 seconds, or until smooth.

Add the remaining soy milk and blend for a further 30 seconds, or until combined. Taste for sweetness and add the maple syrup, if needed.

Put some ice cubes and extra peach slices in four glasses, pour in the smoothie and serve immediately.

HINT:
• The smoothie can be made using dairy products (yoghurt and milk) if preferred.

nutrition per serve: Energy 1006 kJ (240 Cal); Fat 6.8 g; Saturated fat 0.8 g; Protein 9 g; Carbohydrate 34.4 g; Fibre 3.9 g; Cholesterol 1 mg

THIS DRINK IS HIGH IN FIBRE WITH AROUND THREE TIMES THE FIBRE YOU'D GET IN MANY COMMERCIAL FRUIT JUICES. IT ALSO PROVIDES OVER 100 PER CENT OF DAILY NEEDS FOR VITAMIN C.

nutrition per serve: Energy 365 kJ (87 Cal)
Fat 0.3 g
Saturated fat 0 g
Protein 1.5 g
Carbohydrate 17.9 g
Fibre 2 g
Cholesterol 0 mg

# FRESH FRUIT SLUSHY

**90 g (3¼ oz) peeled and cored fresh
pineapple**
**1 banana**
**3 kiwi fruit, peeled and sliced**
**250 ml (9 fl oz/1 cup) unsweetened
tropical fruit juice**
**2 ice cubes**

PREP TIME: 10 MINUTES
COOKING TIME: NIL
SERVES 4

Cut the pineapple and banana into chunks. Put in a blender with the kiwi fruit, fruit juice and ice cubes and blend until smooth. Pour into four glasses and serve.

HINTS:
• If fresh pineapple is not available, replace with tinned sliced pineapple in natural juice.
• Try adding a frozen banana for an extra thick slushy.

# LIGHT MEALS AND LUNCHBOXES

# CHICKEN AND CORN SOUP

THIS CHICKEN SOUP IS EASY TO PREPARE AND IS GREAT FOR A LIGHT MEAL.
IT PROVIDES NIACIN, VITAMIN B6 AND A LITTLE FOLATE AND IRON.

3 corn cobs

1 tbsp vegetable oil

4 spring onions (scallions), finely chopped

2 tsp grated fresh ginger

1 litre (35 fl oz/4 cups) reduced-salt
    chicken stock

1 tbsp reduced-salt soy sauce

½ small barbecued chicken, skin
    discarded, shredded

1 tbsp cornflour (cornstarch)

1 tsp sesame oil

420 g (15 oz) tin creamed corn

thyme sprigs, to garnish

PREP TIME: 15 MINUTES

COOKING TIME: 20 MINUTES

SERVES 6

Cut the corn kernels from the cobs—you will need about 400 g (14 oz/2 cups).

Heat the oil in a large saucepan, add the spring onion and ginger and cook for 1 minute,
or until softened, then add the corn kernels, stock and soy sauce. Bring slowly to the boil,
then reduce the heat and simmer for 10 minutes, or until the kernels are cooked through.
Stir in the chicken.

In a bowl, blend the cornflour with 3 tablespoons water or stock to make a smooth paste.
Add to the soup along with the sesame oil and simmer, stirring continuously, until slightly
thickened. Stir in the creamed corn and heat for 2–3 minutes without allowing the soup to
boil. Serve hot, garnished with thyme sprigs.

HINT:
• If fresh corn is unavailable, use a 440 g (15½ oz) tin of drained corn kernels.

nutrition per serve: Energy 969 kJ (231 Cal); Fat 7.8 g; Saturated fat 1.5 g; Protein 14.7 g;
Carbohydrate 23.7 g; Fibre 3.8 g; Cholesterol 37 mg

# ROAST PUMPKIN SOUP

ROASTING THE PUMPKIN GIVES A STRONGER FLAVOUR TO THIS CLASSIC SOUP, WHICH IS RICH IN BETA-CAROTENE AND POTASSIUM. YOU CAN USE ANY TYPE OF PUMPKIN, ALTHOUGH BUTTERNUT PUMPKIN IS OFTEN POPULAR WITH CHILDREN BECAUSE IT HAS A SWEETER FLAVOUR THAN OTHER VARIETIES.

1.25 kg (2 lb 12 oz) pumpkin (winter
   squash), peeled and cut into chunks
2 tbsp olive oil
1 large onion, chopped
2 tsp ground cumin
1 large carrot, chopped
1 celery stalk, chopped
1 litre (35 fl oz/4 cups) reduced-salt
   chicken or vegetable stock

light sour cream or plain yoghurt,
   to serve
finely chopped parsley, to serve

PREP TIME: 20 MINUTES
COOKING TIME: 55 MINUTES
SERVES 6

Preheat the oven to 180°C (350°F/Gas 4). Put the pumpkin on a greased baking tray and lightly brush with half the oil. Bake for 25 minutes, or until softened and slightly browned.

Heat the remaining oil in a large saucepan over medium heat. Add the onion and cumin and cook for 2 minutes, then add the carrot and celery and cook for a further 3 minutes, stirring frequently. Add the roasted pumpkin and stock, bring to the boil, then reduce the heat and simmer for 20 minutes.

Set the soup aside to cool a little, then purée in batches in a blender or food processor. Return the soup to the pan and gently reheat without boiling. Season to taste. Top with a dollop of sour cream or yoghurt and sprinkle with chopped parsley before serving.

nutrition per serve: Energy 633 kJ (151 Cal); Fat 7.2 g; Saturated fat 1.4 g; Protein 5.4 g; Carbohydrate 15.1 g; Fibre 3 g; Cholesterol 2 mg

# CHICKEN MEATBALL SOUP

**1 spring onion (scallion)**
**375 g (13 oz) minced (ground) chicken**
**875 ml (30 fl oz/3½ cups) reduced-salt**
  **chicken stock**
**2 tbsp frozen peas**
**2 tbsp finely diced carrot**
**60 g (2¼ oz/½ cup) dried pasta shapes**

PREP TIME: 15 MINUTES
COOKING TIME: 10 MINUTES
SERVES 4

Finely chop half the spring onion and thinly slice the remainder. Combine the chicken and finely chopped spring onion until thoroughly mixed, then form the mixture into small balls, about the size of walnuts.

Put the stock in a saucepan and bring to the boil. Add the peas, carrot and pasta shapes. Simmer for 3 minutes, or until the vegetables are tender, then add the reserved sliced spring onion.

Drop the chicken meatballs into the simmering soup. Cook for about 5 minutes, turning the meatballs in the stock so they cook evenly, or until the meatballs turn white and float to the surface and the pasta is cooked through. Skim off any scum from the surface of the soup before serving.

HINT:
• Instead of making the chicken meatballs, you can substitute the minced chicken with the same amount of boneless, skinless chicken breast. Simply cut the chicken into thin slices, place it between two sheets of baking paper and gently pound with a rolling pin to make almost transparent slices. These will cook in seconds in the hot soup.

YOU CAN USE ALPHABET PASTA OR
PASTA SHAPES TO MAKE THIS SOUP
MORE APPEALING TO YOUNGER
CHILDREN. USE MACARONI OR ANY
OTHER PASTA FOR OLDER CHILDREN.

nutrition per serve: Energy 945 kJ (226 Cal)
Fat 8 g
Saturated fat 2.4 g
Protein 23.5 g
Carbohydrate 14.2 g
Fibre 1.3 g
Cholesterol 89 mg

# BUBBLE AND SQUEAK

RICH IN FOLATE AND VITAMIN A, THIS IS A GREAT WAY OF TURNING LEFTOVERS INTO A TASTY AND NUTRITIOUS GLUTEN-FREE MEAL. ADD ANY MEAT FROM DINNER THE NIGHT BEFORE AND YOU WILL BOOST PROTEIN TOO.

150 g (5½ oz/1 cup) cooked potato chunks

150 g (5½ oz/1 cup) cooked pumpkin (winter squash) chunks

75 g (2½ oz/1 cup) grated cabbage, cooked

60 g (2¼ oz/1 cup) small broccoli florets, cooked

4 eggs, beaten

2 chives, snipped

20 g (¾ oz) margarine

PREP TIME: 10 MINUTES
COOKING TIME: 5 MINUTES
SERVES 4

Put the cooked vegetables in a bowl, add the eggs and chives and mix well.

Melt the margarine in a large frying pan and add the vegetable mixture. Cook over medium heat until the underside is golden, then cut into quarters and turn each quarter over in the pan. Cook the mixture for a little longer, or until the surface is golden and the egg has set.

Alternatively, once the underside is set, put the frying pan under a hot grill (broiler) for 1–2 minutes, or until the top is set. Serve with a green salad.

nutrition per serve: Energy 656 kJ (157 Cal); Fat 8.8 g; Saturated fat 2.3 g; Protein 9.5 g; Carbohydrate 8.7 g; Fibre 2.8 g; Cholesterol 187 mg

# SPANISH OMELETTE

THIS OMELETTE IS RICH IN VITAMIN A, FOLATE AND POTASSIUM. IT ALSO
MAKES A GREAT PICNIC FOOD THAT CAN BE SERVED COLD, CUT INTO BITE-
SIZED PIECES FOR CHILDREN OR LARGER WEDGES FOR GROWN-UPS. SERVE
WITH A GREEN SALAD FOR A LIGHT MEAL.

**1 kg (2 lb 4 oz) potatoes**
**50 g (1¾ oz) margarine**
**2 tbsp olive oil**
**2 large red onions, roughly chopped**
**1 garlic clove, crushed**
**2 tbsp finely chopped flat-leaf (Italian)**
**parsley**
**4 eggs, lightly beaten**

PREP TIME: 20 MINUTES
COOKING TIME: 35 MINUTES
SERVES 4–6

Peel and cut the potatoes into small cubes and place in a large saucepan. Cover with
water, bring to the boil and cook, uncovered, for 3 minutes. Remove the pan from the heat
and set aside, covered, for 8 minutes, or until the potato is just tender. Drain well.

Heat the margarine and oil in a deep, non-stick frying pan with a heatproof handle over
medium heat. Add the onion and garlic and cook for 8 minutes, stirring occasionally. Add
the potato and cook for another 5 minutes. Remove the vegetables with a slotted spoon
and transfer them to a large bowl, reserving the oil in the frying pan. Add the parsley and
eggs to the potato and onion and mix until well combined.

Reheat the oil in the frying pan over high heat and add the potato mixture. Reduce the
heat to low and cook, covered, for about 10 minutes, or until the underside of the
omelette is golden. Put the pan under a hot grill (broiler) to brown the top of the omelette.
Cut into wedges to serve.

nutrition per serve (6): Energy 1163 kJ (278 Cal); Fat 15.5 g; Saturated fat 2.9 g; Protein 8.9 g;
Carbohydrate 23.9 g; Fibre 3.5 g; Cholesterol 125 mg

WEDGES OF THIS NOURISHING
FRITTATA MAKE A GREAT
ALTERNATIVE TO SANDWICHES.
MAKE SURE IT IS WELL
WRAPPED AND KEPT CHILLED
IF SENDING TO SCHOOL IN
YOUR CHILD'S LUNCHBOX.

nutrition per serve: Energy 1098 kJ (262 Cal)
Fat 19 g
Saturated fat 5.2 g
Protein 17.2 g
Carbohydrate 4.5 g
Fibre 3.5 g
Cholesterol 245 mg

# LEEK AND ZUCCHINI FRITTATA

**2 tbsp olive oil**

**3 leeks, white part only, thinly sliced**

**2 zucchini (courgettes), cut into matchstick pieces**

**1 garlic clove, crushed**

**5 eggs, lightly beaten**

**4 tbsp grated parmesan cheese**

**4 tbsp grated low-fat cheddar cheese**

PREP TIME: 20 MINUTES

COOKING TIME: 40 MINUTES

SERVES 4

Heat 1 tablespoon of the oil in a small frying pan with a heatproof handle. Add the leek and cook, stirring, over low heat until slightly softened. Cover and cook for 10 minutes, stirring occasionally.

Add the zucchini and garlic and cook for another 10 minutes. Transfer the mixture to a bowl. Set aside to cool, then season with freshly ground black pepper. Add the egg and cheeses and stir to combine.

Heat the remaining oil in the pan, then add the egg mixture and smooth the surface. Cook over low heat for 15 minutes, or until the frittata is almost set. Put the pan under a hot grill (broiler) for 3–5 minutes, or until the top is set and golden. Set the frittata aside for 5 minutes before cutting into wedges. Serve with a green salad.

# RICOTTA AND CORN FRITTERS

THESE FRITTERS WILL MAKE A SIGNIFICANT CONTRIBUTION TO THE CALCIUM AND ZINC NEEDS OF YOUR CHILD, AS WELL AS PROVIDING GOOD QUALITY PROTEIN, VITAL FOR YOUNG BODIES TO GROW.

200 g (7 oz) ricotta cheese

2 eggs

125 ml (4 fl oz/½ cup) reduced-fat milk

75 g (2½ oz/½ cup) wholemeal
   (whole-wheat) self-raising flour

420 g (15 oz) tin corn kernels, drained

3 spring onions (scallions), chopped

2 tbsp snipped chives

canola or olive oil spray

home-made tomato sauce (page 102),
   to serve (optional)

PREP TIME: 10 MINUTES

COOKING TIME: 25 MINUTES

SERVES 4

Put the ricotta, eggs and milk in a bowl and beat together until smooth. Stir in the flour, corn, spring onion and chives.

Spray a non-stick frying pan liberally with oil. Add heaped tablespoons of the corn mixture to the pan, four at a time, and use a spatula to flatten to about 1.5 cm (5/8 in) thick. Cook for 3–4 minutes each side, then remove from the pan and drain on paper towels. Serve the fritters with home-made tomato sauce for dipping if desired.

HINT:
• Swapping regular ricotta cheese for low fat will cut the fat further in this recipe.

nutrition per serve: Energy 1293 kJ (309 Cal); Fat 13.5 g; Saturated fat 6.7 g; Protein 16.9 g; Carbohydrate 27.8 g; Fibre 4.6 g; Cholesterol 132 mg

# CHICKEN AND VEGETABLE OMELETTE ROLLS

POACHING IS A GREAT WAY OF COOKING CHICKEN. THE LIQUID KEEPS THE MEAT MOIST AND TENDER. IF YOU ARE SHORT ON TIME, USE A BARBECUED CHICKEN INSTEAD, WITH THE SKIN REMOVED.

2 x 200 g (7 oz) boneless, skinless chicken breasts, trimmed

8 eggs

1 tbsp sesame seeds

100 g (3½ oz) snow peas (mangetout), cut into matchsticks

1 small cucumber, cut into matchsticks

1 small carrot, cut into matchsticks

**SOY AND SESAME DRESSING**

2 tsp reduced-salt soy sauce

3 tbsp rice vinegar

2 tsp sesame oil

PREP TIME: 15 MINUTES

COOKING TIME: 20 MINUTES

SERVES 6

Arrange the chicken breasts in a single layer in a large shallow saucepan. Add enough cold water to cover by about 3 cm (1¼ in). Bring to a very slow simmer, then cook over low heat for 10 minutes. Turn the heat off and allow the chicken to cool in the cooking liquid.

To make the soy and sesame dressing, combine the ingredients together in a bowl and set aside. Finely shred the cooled chicken, pour over the dressing and gently toss to coat the chicken.

Preheat the grill (broiler) to medium. Whisk the eggs and 1 tablespoon water together in a bowl.

Heat a lightly oiled 20 cm (8 in) non-stick frying pan over medium heat. When the pan is hot, pour in one-sixth of the egg mixture and swirl it around the base and side, then quickly remove from the heat and sprinkle with some of the sesame seeds. Put the pan under the grill for about 1 minute, or until the omelette is lightly browned. Slide the omelette onto a large plate and cover with foil to keep warm. Repeat with the remaining egg mixture and sesame seeds to make six omelettes in total.

Divide the chicken, snow peas, cucumber and carrot among the omelettes, then fold in the sides to enclose the filling. Serve with a green salad.

nutrition per serve: Energy 869 kJ (208 Cal); Fat 10.8 g; Saturated fat 2.9 g; Protein 24.4 g; Carbohydrate 2.5 g; Fibre 1 g; Cholesterol 293 mg

**65**

# SWEET POTATO AND RED LENTIL DIP

250 g (9 oz) orange sweet potato, peeled
   and roughly chopped
2 tsp olive oil
1 small red onion, finely chopped
1 garlic clove, crushed
1 tsp grated fresh ginger
1 tbsp Thai red curry paste
200 g (7 oz) tinned no-added-salt diced
   tomatoes

100 g (3½ oz/½ cup) split red lentils,
   rinsed (see Hint)
375 ml (13 fl oz/1½ cups) reduced-salt
   chicken stock

PREP TIME: 15 MINUTES
COOKING TIME: 35 MINUTES
SERVES 6–8

Put the sweet potato in a steamer and cover with a lid. Sit the steamer over a wok or saucepan of boiling water and steam for 15 minutes, or until tender. Transfer to a bowl, cool and mash roughly with a fork.

Heat the oil in a saucepan over medium heat and cook the onion for 2 minutes, or until softened. Add the garlic, ginger and curry paste and stir for 30 seconds.

Add the tomatoes, lentils and stock to the pan. Bring to the boil, then reduce the heat to low and simmer, stirring often, for 15 minutes, or until the mixture thickens and the lentils have softened but are still intact. Spoon the mixture into a bowl, refrigerate until cold, then carefully stir into the mashed sweet potato with a fork. Season to taste with freshly ground black pepper. Serve with crusty bread for dipping.

HINT:
• If you are using whole red lentils for this recipe instead of split lentils, increase the cooking time to 30 minutes and cover the pan with a lid.

SERVE THIS FIBRE-RICH
NUTRITIOUS DIP WITH PITTA
BREAD WEDGES, PARMESAN
GRISSINI (PAGE 71) OR
VEGETABLE STICKS. IT ALSO
MAKES A GOOD ACCOMPANIMENT
TO A VEGETARIAN MAIN MEAL
WITH RICE.

nutrition per serve (8): Energy 347 kJ (83 Cal)
Fat 1.9 g
Saturated fat 0.3 g
Protein 4.7 g
Carbohydrate 10.7 g
Fibre 2.8 g
Cholesterol 1 mg

# CHICKPEA AND CANNELLINI BEAN DIP

THIS TASTY LOW-GI DIP IS AN EXCELLENT SOURCE OF FIBRE AND SLOWLY DIGESTED CARBOHYDRATES, AND IS A GREAT WAY OF 'SNEAKING' LEGUMES INTO YOUR CHILD'S DIET. SERVE WITH VEGETABLE STICKS FOR DIPPING.

400 g (14 oz) tin cannellini beans, drained and rinsed
400 g (14 oz) tin chickpeas, drained and rinsed
1½ tsp ground cumin
3 garlic cloves, crushed
2 tbsp chopped flat-leaf (Italian) parsley
3 tbsp lemon juice

1 tsp grated lemon zest
1 tbsp tahini

PREP TIME: 10 MINUTES
COOKING TIME: NIL
SERVES 8

Place all the ingredients in a food processor and process for 30 seconds. With the motor still running, slowly add 3 tablespoons hot water to the processor in a thin stream, adding just enough so the mixture is smooth and 'dippable'.

Serve at room temperature with vegetable sticks and pitta crisps.

HINT:
• When using tinned chickpeas and beans, make sure you drain and rinse them well to remove some of the salt.

nutrition per serve: Energy 329 kJ (79 Cal); Fat 2.5 g; Saturated fat 0.3 g; Protein 4.2 g; Carbohydrate 8.9 g; Fibre 4 g; Cholesterol 0 mg

# HUMMUS

THIS POPULAR DIP IS DELICIOUS ON BREAD AS A SUBSTITUTE FOR
MARGARINE, OR GREAT AS AN AFTER-SCHOOL SNACK WITH SOME CARROT,
CUCUMBER AND CELERY STICKS FOR DIPPING. IT IS ALSO DELICIOUS AS A
FILLING WITH TABOULEH, ROLLED UP IN PITTA BREAD FOR SCHOOL LUNCHES.

**225 g (8 oz/1 cup) dried chickpeas**
**2 tbsp tahini**
**4 garlic cloves, crushed**
**80 ml (2½ fl oz/⅓ cup) lemon juice,**
  **plus extra to taste (optional)**
**2 tbsp olive oil**
**2 tsp ground cumin**
**pinch of cayenne pepper**

**ground paprika, to garnish**
**1 tbsp chopped parsley**

PREP TIME: 20 MINUTES + OVERNIGHT
  SOAKING
COOKING TIME: 1¼ HOURS
SERVES 6–8

Put the chickpeas in a large bowl, cover with water and leave to soak overnight. Drain
and rinse well.

Transfer the chickpeas to a large saucepan and cover with cold water. Bring to the boil,
then reduce the heat and simmer for 1¼ hours, or until the chickpeas are very tender,
occasionally skimming any froth from the surface. Drain well, reserving about 250 ml
(9 fl oz/1 cup) of the cooking liquid, and leave the chickpeas until cool enough to handle.
Pick over for any loose skins and discard.

Process the chickpeas, tahini, garlic, lemon juice, olive oil, cumin, cayenne pepper and
½ teaspoon salt in a food processor until thick and smooth. With the motor still running,
gradually add about 185 ml (6 fl oz/¾ cup) of the reserved cooking liquid to form a smooth
creamy purée. Add extra lemon juice, to taste, if necessary.

Transfer the hummus to a flat bowl or plate, sprinkle with paprika and scatter the parsley
over the top.

HINT:
• If preferred, use 2 x 400 g (14 oz) tins of chickpeas instead of the dried chickpeas. The
  tinned chickpeas only need to be drained and rinsed well, then can be added to the
  food processor along with the other ingredients.

nutrition per serve (8): Energy 763 kJ (182 Cal); Fat 9.5 g; Saturated fat 1.2 g; Protein 6.7 g;
Carbohydrate 12.9 g; Fibre 6 g; Cholesterol 0 mg

THIS RECIPE IS GREAT FOR
WEEKENDS OR RAINY DAYS WHEN
KIDS CAN LEND A HAND ROLLING
AND CUTTING THE DOUGH. THESE
GRISSINI GO WELL WITH DIPS OR
PACKED AS A CRUNCHY SNACK IN
THE LUNCHBOX.

nutrition per grissini: Energy 180 kJ (43 Cal)
Fat 1.3 g
Saturated fat 0.5 g
Protein 1.7 g
Carbohydrate 5.8 g
Fibre 0.3 g
Cholesterol 2 mg

# PARMESAN GRISSINI

**1 tsp instant dried yeast**
**pinch of caster (superfine) sugar**
**1 tbsp extra virgin olive oil**
**250 g (9 oz/2 cups) strong flour**
**60 g (2¼ oz/⅔ cup) grated parmesan**
  **cheese**

PREP TIME: 20 MINUTES + 1¼ HOURS
  STANDING
COOKING TIME: 20 MINUTES
MAKES 32

Put 170 ml (5½ fl oz/⅔ cup) warm water in a small bowl and sprinkle over the yeast and sugar. Stir to dissolve the sugar, then leave in a draught-free place for 10–15 minutes, or until the yeast is foamy. Stir in the olive oil.

Put the flour into a large bowl, add the grated parmesan and ½ teaspoon salt and stir to combine well. Pour in the yeast mixture and stir until a dough forms. Turn the dough out onto a lightly floured work surface and knead for 5 minutes, or until the dough is smooth and elastic.

Grease a large bowl with oil, then transfer the dough to the bowl, turning the dough to coat in the oil. Cover with plastic wrap and leave to rise in a draught-free place for 1 hour, or until the dough has doubled in size.

Preheat the oven to 200°C (400°F/Gas 6). Lightly grease two baking trays.

Knock back the dough by punching it gently, then turn out onto a floured work surface and cut in half. Roll out one piece of dough to form a 20 x 16 cm (8 x 6¼ in) rectangle, then cut into sixteen 1 cm (½ in) wide strips. Using your hands, gently roll each strip to form a 22–24 cm (8½–9½ in) long stick, then place on the prepared tray. Repeat for the second piece of dough. Bake for 17–20 minutes, or until golden and crisp, swapping the trays halfway through to ensure even cooking. Transfer to a wire rack to cool.

HINTS:
- If making the grissini for your children's lunches, you might like to make them shorter so they fit into their lunchboxes.
- Grissini will keep, stored in an airtight container, for up to 7 days. Re-crisp in a 180°C (350°F/Gas 4) oven for 5 minutes if they become soft.

# HAM AND PINEAPPLE ROLLS

2 bread rolls
1 tbsp light cream cheese spread
50 g (1¾ oz) ham (2 slices)
60 g (2¼ oz) fresh pineapple
(about 2 slices), thinly sliced

PREP TIME: 5 MINUTES
COOKING TIME: NIL
MAKES 2 ROLLS

Cut the bread rolls in half and spread with the cream cheese. Top with the sliced ham and pineapple and finish with the bread roll top.

nutrition per roll: Energy 1191 kJ (285 Cal); Fat 6.1 g; Saturated fat 2.2 g; Protein 13.2 g; Carbohydrate 42.3 g; Fibre 3.4 g; Cholesterol 21 mg

# CHICKEN, MAYO AND APPLE SANDWICH

90 g (3¼ oz/½ cup) finely chopped,
skinless cooked chicken
1 tbsp low-fat mayonnaise
½ small red apple, peeled, finely diced
3 fresh dates, finely chopped
4 slices bread

PREP TIME: 10 MINUTES
COOKING TIME: NIL
MAKES 2 SANDWICHES

To make the filling, combine the chicken, mayonnaise, apple and dates in a bowl. Spread the filling evenly over two of the slices of bread and top with the remaining bread.

nutrition per sandwich: Energy 1303 kJ (311 Cal); Fat 6.5 g; Saturated fat 1.5 g; Protein 18.2 g; Carbohydrate 43.4 g; Fibre 3.7 g; Cholesterol 47 mg

HINT:
• To make sandwich rolls, remove the crusts from the bread, then use a rolling pin to roll out and flatten the bread. Spread the chicken mixture over each slice of bread and roll up to enclose the filling.

# TUNA, AVOCADO AND CHEESE WRAPS

**95 g (3¼ oz) tin sandwich tuna in spring water, drained**
**2 tortillas**
**1 tbsp low-fat mayonnaise**
**½ small avocado, thinly sliced**
**4 tbsp grated low-fat cheddar cheese**

PREP TIME: 10 MINUTES
COOKING TIME: NIL
MAKES 2 WRAPS

Put the drained tuna in a bowl and finely flake with a fork. Spread the tortillas evenly with the mayonnaise, then top half of each tortilla with the flaked tuna, avocado slices and cheese. Roll up, starting from the filled side, to enclose the filling. Cut in half to serve.

nutrition per wrap: Energy 1260 kJ (301 Cal); Fat 17.1 g; Saturated fat 5 g; Protein 23.6 g; Carbohydrate 12.6 g; Fibre 1.4 g; Cholesterol 30 mg

# SALMON, CARROT AND CUCUMBER PITTA ROLLS

**105 g (3½ oz) tin pink salmon in spring water, drained**
**2 pitta breads**
**2 tsp margarine**
**½ small Lebanese (short) cucumber, thinly sliced**
**1 small carrot, finely grated**

PREP TIME: 10 MINUTES
COOKING TIME: NIL
MAKES 2

Remove the bones from the salmon and finely flake the salmon into a bowl. Spread the pitta breads with the margarine, top half of each bread with the salmon, cucumber and carrot. Roll up to serve.

nutrition per roll: Energy 1292 kJ (309 Cal); Fat 7.5 g; Saturated fat 1.6 g; Protein 15.9 g; Carbohydrate 42.3 g; Fibre 3.3 g; Cholesterol 31 mg

# CHEESE TABOULEH WRAPS

**2 pieces mountain bread**
**1 tbsp low-fat mayonnaise**
**4 slices low-fat cheddar cheese**

**TABOULEH**
**45 g (1½ oz/¼ cup) couscous**
**1 tbsp olive oil**
**60 ml (2 fl oz/¼ cup) reduced-salt**
**chicken stock**

**1 tbsp chopped flat-leaf (Italian) parsley**
**½ small tomato, finely chopped**
**2–3 tsp lemon juice**

PREP TIME: 10 MINUTES
COOKING TIME: 5 MINUTES
MAKES 2 WRAPS

Spread the bread with mayonnaise and top each with two slices of cheese.

Put the couscous in a bowl, add ½ teaspoon of the oil and rub the oil into the couscous grains with your fingers to coat evenly. Put the stock in a saucepan and bring to the boil. Add the stock to the couscous, cover and set aside for 5 minutes. Fluff up the grains with a fork and add the parsley, tomato, remaining olive oil and lemon juice to taste.

Spread the couscous over the top of the cheese, leaving a 2 cm (¾ in) gap at one short end. Roll up to enclose the filling. Cut in half to serve.

THESE TASTY NUTRITIOUS WRAPS
ARE RICH IN CALCIUM FROM THE
CHEESE, AND BETA-CAROTENE,
FOLATE AND VITAMIN C FROM
THE TABOULEH.

nutrition per wrap: Energy 1407 kJ (336 Cal)

Fat 13.2 g

Saturated fat 3.4 g

Protein 20 g

Carbohydrate 33 g

Fibre 1.9 g

Cholesterol 16 mg

# CORN AND HAM MINI MUFFINS

SAVOURY MUFFINS ARE A GOOD WAY TO GET EXTRA VEGETABLES INTO YOUR CHILD'S DIET. IF YOU PREFER, USE WHOLEMEAL (WHOLE-WHEAT) FLOUR INSTEAD OF WHITE FLOUR. A LITTLE EXTRA MILK MAY BE REQUIRED AS WHOLEMEAL FLOUR ABSORBS MORE LIQUID.

canola or olive oil spray
125 g (4½ oz/1 cup) self-raising flour
40 g (1½ oz/¼ cup) chopped ham
60 g (2¼ oz/⅓ cup) tinned corn kernels, drained
¼ red capsicum (pepper), seeded and finely chopped
2 tsp chopped parsley

60 g (2¼ oz) margarine, melted
125 ml (4 fl oz/½ cup) reduced-fat milk
1 egg
1 tbsp sesame seeds

PREP TIME: 10 MINUTES
COOKING TIME: 20 MINUTES
MAKES 24

Preheat the oven to 210°C (415°C/Gas 6–7). Lightly spray two 12-hole mini muffin tins with oil.

Sift the flour into a large bowl. Add the chopped ham, corn, capsicum and parsley and stir to combine.

In a small bowl, combine the melted margarine, milk and egg. Make a well in the centre of the flour mixture and pour in the milk mixture. Mix the dough lightly with a fork or rubber spatula until the ingredients are just combined. Do not overmix; the batter should be quite lumpy.

Spoon the mixture into the prepared tins. Sprinkle the muffins with the sesame seeds, then bake for 15–20 minutes, or until golden. Cool on a wire rack.

HINT:
• Try adding other vegetables instead of the corn and capsicum, such as ½ grated carrot and zucchini (courgette). For a vegetarian option, replace the ham with chopped semi-dried (sun-blushed) tomatoes.

nutrition per muffin: Energy 205 kJ (49 Cal); Fat 2.5 g; Saturated fat 0.5 g; Protein 1.6 g; Carbohydrate 4.9 g; Fibre 0.4 g; Cholesterol 9 mg

# CARROT AND APRICOT MUFFINS

THESE VERSATILE MUFFINS ARE GREAT AS A SNACK OR LIGHT MEAL AT ANY
TIME OF DAY. BEING LIGHT AND PORTABLE, THEY MAKE A NICE ADDITION TO
PACKED LUNCHES OR PICNIC HAMPERS. MUFFINS CAN BE FROZEN AND THEN
PULLED OUT OF THE FREEZER FOR THE OCCASIONAL TREAT.

canola or olive oil spray
225 g (8 oz/1½ cups) stoneground
    self-raising flour
½ tsp bicarbonate of soda (baking soda)
1 tsp mixed spice
50 g (1¾ oz/½ cup) rolled barley
60 g (2¼ oz/⅓ cup) soft brown sugar
75 g (2½ oz/½ cup) dried apricots,
    chopped
155 g (5½ oz/1 cup) grated carrot

1 egg
250 ml (9 fl oz/1 cup) reduced-fat milk
125 ml (4 fl oz/½ cup) unsweetened apple
    juice
2 tbsp canola oil

PREP TIME: 20 MINUTES
COOKING TIME: 25 MINUTES
MAKES 12

Preheat the oven to 170°C (325°F/Gas 3). Lightly spray a 12-hole standard muffin tin
with oil.

Sift the flour, bicarbonate of soda and mixed spice into a large bowl, then return the husks
to the bowl (see Hints). Stir in the rolled barley, brown sugar, apricots and carrot. Make a
well in the centre.

Whisk together the egg, milk, apple juice and oil and stir into the flour mixture until just
combined. Do not overmix; the batter should be quite lumpy.

Spoon the mixture evenly into the muffin holes. Bake for 25 minutes, or until firm to touch
and golden brown. Leave in the tin for 5 minutes, then turn out onto a wire rack to cool.

HINTS:
• Organic brands of stoneground flour have husks in them, which can be returned to the
  bowl after sifting, for added fibre.
• You can also make these muffins in mini muffin tins to make smaller treats for children.
  Reduce the cooking time to 15–20 minutes.

nutrition per muffin: Energy 686 kJ (164 Cal); Fat 4.3 g; Saturated fat 0.6 g; Protein 4 g;
Carbohydrate 27 g; Fibre 2.1 g; Cholesterol 17 mg

THESE DELICIOUS MUFFINS ARE
VERY EASY TO MAKE, SO OFFER
A GREAT OPPORTUNITY FOR
CHILDREN TO HELP PREPARE FOOD
FOR THEIR OWN LUNCHBOXES.

nutrition per muffin: Energy 567 kJ (135 Cal)

Fat 4.5 g

Saturated fat 0.7 g

Protein 3 g

Carbohydrate 20.4 g

Fibre 1.3 g

Cholesterol 13 mg

# EASY APPLE MUFFINS

250 g (9 oz/1 cup) low-fat plain yoghurt
100 g (3½ oz/1 cup) rolled (porridge) oats
3 tbsp oil
80 g (2¾ oz/⅓ cup) caster (superfine) sugar
1 egg
125 g (4½ oz/1 cup) self-raising flour, sifted
1 tsp baking powder
½ tsp ground cinnamon

2 granny smith apples, peeled, cored and diced
60 g (2¼ oz/½ cup) sultanas (golden raisins)

PREP TIME: 10 MINUTES
COOKING TIME: 25 MINUTES
MAKES 16

Preheat the oven to 180°C (350°F/Gas 4). Line 16 holes of two standard muffin tins with paper cases.

Combine the yoghurt, oats, oil, sugar and egg in a bowl. Gently stir in the sifted flour, baking powder and cinnamon with the apple and sultanas. Do not overmix; the batter should be quite lumpy.

Spoon the mixture evenly into the paper cases and bake for 15 minutes, then swap the position of the tins and bake for a further 5–7 minutes, or until golden brown and a skewer comes out clean when inserted into the centre. Leave to cool in the tins for 5 minutes before turning out onto a wire rack.

HINT:
• Muffins can be made with any number of delicious fruit-based combinations. Try berry combinations, or pear and dates can make a tasty alternative.

# PANCAKES

PANCAKES MAKE A NICE TREAT FOR AFTERNOON TEA OR CAN BE SPREAD WITH
A LITTLE JAM AND PACKED FOR SCHOOL LUNCHES.

**185 g (6½ oz/1½ cups) self-raising flour**
**1 tsp baking powder**
**2 tbsp caster (superfine) sugar**
**2 eggs, lightly beaten**
**250 ml (9 fl oz/1 cup) reduced-fat milk**
**60 g (2¼ oz) margarine, melted**

PREP TIME: 5 MINUTES + 20 MINUTES
     STANDING
COOKING TIME: 15–20 MINUTES
MAKES 9 PANCAKES

Sift the flour, baking powder, sugar and a pinch of salt into a bowl and make a well in the centre. Mix together the eggs, milk and melted margarine and pour into the well all at once, whisking to form a smooth batter. Cover the bowl with plastic wrap and set aside for 20 minutes.

Heat a frying pan and brush lightly with melted margarine or oil. Pour 60 ml (2 fl oz/¼ cup) of the batter into the pan and swirl gently to create a pancake about 10 cm (4 in) in diameter. Cook over low heat for 1 minute, or until the underside is golden. Turn the pancake over and cook the other side for about 10 seconds, then transfer to a plate and keep warm while cooking the remaining batter.

Serve the pancakes warm or cold, spread with a little margarine or topped with low-fat vanilla yoghurt and slices of fruit, such as strawberries or bananas.

nutrition per pancake: Energy 683 kJ (163 Cal); Fat 6.1 g; Saturated fat 1.4 g; Protein 4.9 g; Carbohydrate 22 g; Fibre 0.9 g; Cholesterol 44 mg

# WHOLEMEAL BANANA BREAD

THIS BANANA BREAD IS LOWER IN FAT AND HIGHER IN FIBRE THAN REGULAR
VARIETIES BECAUSE THERE IS LESS OIL AND ADDED WHEAT BRAN AND
WHOLEMEAL FLOUR. CUT INTO THICK SLICES AND FREEZE, SO YOU WILL
ALWAYS HAVE SOME ON STANDBY FOR SNACKS OR LUNCHES.

95 g (3¼ oz/½ cup) soft brown sugar
1 egg
200 g (7 oz) low-fat vanilla fromage frais
   or whipped yoghurt
2 tbsp canola oil
2 ripe bananas, mashed, to give about
   240 g (8½ oz/1 cup)
30 g (1 oz/¼ cup) sultanas (golden raisins)
125 g (4½ oz/1 cup) self-raising flour
35 g (1¼ oz/¼ cup) wholemeal
   (whole-wheat) self-raising flour

½ tsp bicarbonate of soda (baking soda)
2 tbsp unprocessed wheat bran
1 tsp ground cinnamon
½ tsp ground nutmeg

PREP TIME: 15 MINUTES
COOKING TIME: 50 MINUTES
MAKES 10–12 SLICES

Preheat the oven to 160°C (315°F/Gas 2–3). Line the base of a 20.5 x 10.5 cm (8 x 4 in)
loaf (bar) tin with baking paper.

Place the sugar, egg, fromage frais and oil in a large bowl and whisk until well combined.
Fold in the banana and sultanas, then fold in the sifted flours, bicarbonate of soda, wheat
bran, cinnamon and nutmeg.

Spoon the mixture into the prepared tin and bake for 50 minutes, or until cooked through
when tested with a skewer. Serve warm or cold with low-fat yoghurt for an added calcium
boost. The banana bread is also delicious toasted.

nutrition per slice (12): Energy 656 kJ (157 Cal); Fat 3.9 g; Saturated fat 0.6 g; Protein 3.5 g;
Carbohydrate 26.4 g; Fibre 1.8 g; Cholesterol 16 mg

# SNACK BARS

**60 g (2¼ oz/2 cups) puffed rice cereal**
**150 g (5½ oz/1½ cups) wholegrain rolled**
   **(porridge) oats**
**30 g (1 oz/¼ cup) sunflower seeds**
**40 g (1½ oz/¼ cup) sesame seeds**
**200 g (7 oz) packet dried fruit medley**
**40 g (1½ oz/⅓ cup) plain (all-purpose)**
   **flour**
**175 g (6 oz/¼ cup) honey**

PREP TIME: 10 MINUTES
COOKING TIME: 25 MINUTES
MAKES 16–20

Preheat the oven to 180°C (350°F/Gas 4). Line the base and two long sides of a 29 x 19 cm (11½ x 7½ in) rectangular cake tin with baking paper.

Place the puffed rice cereal, oats, sunflower seeds, sesame seeds, dried fruit and flour in a bowl and mix together well.

Place the honey and 2 tablespoons water in a small saucepan and heat gently over medium heat for 1–2 minutes, or until runny. Stir the syrup into the dry ingredients and mix thoroughly to coat in the honey.

Press the mixture firmly into the prepared tin. Place a sheet of baking paper over the mixture and use the back of a spoon or a measuring cup to spread it evenly. Remove the top sheet of baking paper and bake for 20 minutes, or until golden brown. Leave to cool and crisp in the tin before lifting out and cutting into fingers. Store in an airtight container in the refrigerator.

WHILE BETTER THAN MANY
COMMERCIALLY MADE MUESLI BARS
THESE BARS ARE STILL HIGH IN
SUGAR FROM THE DRIED FRUIT AND
HONEY. TEAM THEM WITH A DRINK
OF WATER OR MILK TO CLEAR STICKY
RESIDUES AND PROTECT TEETH.

nutrition per bar (20): Energy 509 kJ (122 Cal)
Fat 2.6 g
Saturated fat 0.3 g
Protein 2.3 g
Carbohydrate 21.8 g
Fibre 1.8 g
Cholesterol 0 mg

# CHOCOLATE WHEAT BRAN BISCUITS

CHILDREN OFTEN DON'T EAT ENOUGH FIBRE, BUT WHAT A MORE ENTICING WAY TO GET IT THAN WITH CHOCOLATE. EXPERIMENT WITH THE DIFFERENT TYPES OF BRANS—WHEAT, RICE, OAT OR BARLEY TO FIND THE TYPE YOUR FAMILY ENJOY MOST. ENJOY THESE BISCUITS IN MODERATION OR AS A TREAT.

90 g (3¼ oz) margarine
60 g (2¼ oz/⅓ cup) soft brown sugar
1 egg
20 g (¾ oz/¼ cup) unprocessed wheat bran
25 g (1 oz/¼ cup) desiccated coconut
75 g (2½ oz/½ cup) stoneground wholemeal (whole-wheat) self-raising flour

110 g (3¾ oz/¾ cup) stoneground plain (all-purpose) flour
80 ml (2½ fl oz/⅓ cup) reduced-fat milk
90 g (3¼ oz/½ cup) dark chocolate chips

PREP TIME: 20 MINUTES
COOKING TIME: 15 MINUTES
MAKES 18

Preheat the oven to 180°C (350°F/Gas 4). Line a large baking tray with baking paper.

Put the margarine and sugar in a bowl and beat with electric beaters for 1–2 minutes until creamy. Add the egg and beat well. Stir in the wheat bran and coconut.

Sift the flours into a bowl, then return any husks to the bowl. Fold a little at a time into the egg mixture, alternating with the milk. Set aside for 5 minutes to absorb a little moisture.

Roll tablespoons of the mixture into balls and place on the prepared tray. Flatten to 5 cm (2 in), then press lightly with a floured fork. Bake for 12–15 minutes, or until golden brown. Leave to cool on the tray before transferring to a wire rack.

Melt the chocolate in the microwave or in a small bowl set over a saucepan of simmering water. Spoon the chocolate into the corner of a small plastic bag and snip a small hole. Drizzle the chocolate over the biscuits and leave to set. The biscuits can be stored in an airtight container for up to 5 days.

nutrition per biscuit: Energy 502 kJ (120 Cal); Fat 6.2 g; Saturated fat 2.8 g; Protein 2.1 g; Carbohydrate 13.5 g; Fibre 1.5 g; Cholesterol 11 mg

# FRUITY BRAN LOAF

THIS LOAF IS LOW GI AND LOW IN FAT AND CAN BE ENJOYED AS A SNACK OR FOR SCHOOL LUNCHES. TRY IT TOASTED, TOPPED WITH A LITTLE FRUIT SPREAD OR YOGHURT.

60 g (2¼ oz/½ cup) chopped dried pears
60 g (2¼ oz/½ cup) chopped dried peaches
125 g (4½ oz/1 cup) dried fruit medley or chopped dried apricots
70 g (2½ oz/1 cup) processed wheat bran cereal
100 g (3½ oz/½ cup) soft brown sugar
375 ml (13 fl oz/1½ cups) reduced-fat milk

canola or olive oil spray
185 g (6½ oz/1¼ cups) stoneground self-raising flour
1 tsp mixed spice

PREP TIME: 15 MINUTES + 1 HOUR STANDING
COOKING TIME: 50 MINUTES
MAKES 10–12 SLICES

Put the pears, peaches, fruit medley, wheat bran cereal, brown sugar and milk in a large bowl. Stir to combine and set aside for 1 hour until the bran has softened.

Preheat the oven to 180°C (350°F/Gas 4). Spray a 19.5 x 9.5 cm (7½ x 3¾ in) loaf (bar) tin with oil, then line the base with baking paper.

Sift the flour and mixed spice into a bowl, then return any husks to the bowl. Stir into the fruit mixture and thoroughly combine. Spoon the mixture into the prepared tin and smooth the surface.

Bake for 45–50 minutes, or until cooked when tested with a metal skewer. Leave in the tin for 10 minutes, then turn out onto a wire rack to cool completely. Serve thickly sliced. The loaf will keep refrigerated for up to 1 week and frozen for up to 1 month.

nutrition per slice (12): Energy 651 kJ (156 Cal); Fat 1 g; Saturated fat 0.4 g; Protein 4.2 g; Carbohydrate 30.7 g; Fibre 4.2 g; Cholesterol 2 mg

# RICE AND PASTA

THIS NO-FUSS MEAL IS MADE EVEN
MORE SO BY THE ADDITION OF A
BARBECUED CHICKEN—WITHOUT
THE SKIN. GOOD FOR BODY-BUILDING
PROTEIN AND B VITAMINS, SERVE
THIS PILAF WITH STEAMED CARROT
STICKS, SNOW PEAS AND BROCCOLI.

nutrition per serve: Energy 1463 kJ (350 Cal)

Fat 10.2 g

Saturated fat 2.3 g

Protein 18.2 g

Carbohydrate 45.2 g

Fibre 1.6 g

Cholesterol 48 mg

# CHICKEN PILAF

½ large barbecued chicken
50 g (1¾ oz) margarine
1 onion, finely chopped
2 garlic cloves, crushed
300 g (10½ oz/1½ cups) basmati rice
1 tbsp currants
2 tbsp finely chopped dried apricots
1 tsp ground cinnamon
pinch of ground cardamom

750 ml (26 fl oz/3 cups) reduced-salt
    chicken stock
1 small handful coriander (cilantro) leaves,
    chopped

PREP TIME: 15 MINUTES
COOKING TIME: 20 MINUTES
SERVES 6

Remove the skin and any fat from the chicken and shred the meat into bite-sized pieces.

Melt the margarine in a large, deep frying pan over medium heat. Add the onion and garlic and cook for 2 minutes. Add the rice, currants, apricots and spices and stir until well coated. Pour in the stock and bring to the boil. Reduce the heat to low and simmer, covered, for 15 minutes. Add a little water if it starts to dry out.

Add the chicken and stir for 1–2 minutes, or until heated through, then stir in the coriander just before serving.

# FRIED RICE

USING FROZEN VEGETABLES WON'T COMPROMISE YOUR FAMILY'S NUTRITION.
THAT'S BECAUSE THEIR COOKING AND FREEZING ARE SO QUICK THAT THE
LOSS OF IMPORTANT NUTRIENTS IS ONLY SMALL.

2 tbsp peanut oil

2 eggs, well beaten

4 rindless bacon slices, chopped

2 tsp finely grated fresh ginger

1 garlic clove, crushed

6 spring onions (scallions), finely chopped

50 g (1¾ oz) red capsicum (pepper),
  seeded and diced

1 tsp sesame oil

750 g (1 lb 10 oz/4 cups) cooked, cold,
  long-grain white rice (see Hint)

100 g (3½ oz/⅔ cup) frozen peas, thawed

115 g (4 oz/⅔ cup) cooked, chopped
  skinless chicken

2 tbsp reduced-salt soy sauce

PREP TIME: 25 MINUTES

COOKING TIME: 10 MINUTES

SERVES 6

Heat a large heavy-based wok until very hot, add about 2 teaspoons of the peanut oil and swirl to coat the base and side. Pour in the eggs and swirl to coat the side of the wok. Cook until just set. Remove the egg from the wok, roll up and set aside. Add the remaining peanut oil to the wok and stir-fry the bacon for 2 minutes. Add the ginger, garlic, spring onion and capsicum and stir-fry for 2 minutes.

Add the sesame oil and rice to the wok. Stir-fry until the rice is heated through.

Cut the egg into thin strips and add to the wok along with the peas and chicken. Cover and steam for 1 minute, or until heated through. Stir in the soy sauce. Serve the rice with stir-fried vegetables.

HINT:
• White rice almost triples in bulk during cooking, so you will need about 250 g (9 oz/1¼ cups) uncooked rice to give 750 g (1 lb 10 oz/4 cups) cooked rice.

nutrition per serve: Energy 1480 kJ (354 Cal); Fat 13.3 g; Saturated fat 3.3 g; Protein 18.6 g; Carbohydrate 37.7 g; Fibre 2 g; Cholesterol 99 mg

# CARROT AND PUMPKIN RISOTTO

THIS IS A GREAT WEEKNIGHT DISH FOR WHEN YOU HAVEN'T PLANNED AHEAD, AS YOU'LL FIND YOU'VE PROBABLY GOT MOST OF THE INGREDIENTS IN YOUR CUPBOARD AND REFRIGERATOR.

30 g (1 oz) margarine

1 onion, finely chopped

250 g (9 oz) peeled pumpkin (winter squash), cut into small cubes

2 carrots, cut into small cubes

1.75–2 litres (61–70 fl oz/7–8 cups) reduced-salt vegetable stock

440 g (15½ oz/2 cups) risotto rice

50 g (1¾ oz/½ cup) grated parmesan cheese

¼ tsp ground nutmeg

PREP TIME: 15 MINUTES

COOKING TIME: 35 MINUTES

SERVES 6

Heat the margarine in a large heavy-based saucepan. Add the onion and fry for 2 minutes, or until soft. Add the pumpkin and carrot and cook for 6–8 minutes, or until tender.

Put the stock in a separate saucepan and keep at simmering point.

Add the rice to the vegetables and cook for 1 minute, stirring constantly, then ladle in enough hot stock to cover the rice and stir well. Reduce the heat and add more stock as it is absorbed, stirring frequently. Cook for another 25 minutes, or until the rice is tender and creamy.

Remove the pan from the heat, stir in the parmesan and nutmeg and season with freshly ground black pepper. Fork through to combine. Cover and leave the risotto for 5 minutes before serving. Serve with a green salad.

nutrition per serve: Energy 1638 kJ (391 Cal); Fat 7.7 g; Saturated fat 2.9 g; Protein 10.1 g; Carbohydrate 68.5 g; Fibre 2.3 g; Cholesterol 8 mg

# PEA AND HAM RISOTTO

1 tbsp olive oil

1 celery stalk, chopped

2 tbsp chopped flat-leaf (Italian) parsley

70 g (2½ oz) sliced ham, chopped

250 g (9 oz/1⅔ cups) fresh or frozen peas

875 ml (30 fl oz/3½ cups) reduced-salt
  chicken stock

60 g (2¼ oz) margarine

1 onion, chopped

440 g (15½ oz/2 cups) risotto rice

35 g (1¼ oz/⅓ cup) grated parmesan
  cheese, plus extra shavings, to garnish

PREP TIME: 25 MINUTES

COOKING TIME: 45 MINUTES

SERVES 6

Heat the oil in a frying pan over medium heat, add the celery and parsley and season with freshly ground black pepper. Cook for a few minutes to soften the celery, then add the ham and stir for 1 minute. Add the peas and 60 ml (2 fl oz/¼ cup) of the stock, bring to the boil, then reduce the heat and simmer, uncovered, until almost all the liquid has evaporated. Set aside.

Put the remaining stock and 750 ml (26 fl oz/3 cups) water in a separate saucepan and keep at simmering point.

Heat the margarine in a large heavy-based saucepan. Add the onion and stir until softened, then add the rice and stir well. Add 125 ml (4 fl oz/½ cup) of the hot stock to the rice. Stir constantly over low heat with a wooden spoon until all the stock has been absorbed. Repeat the process until all the stock has been added and the rice is creamy and tender, about 25 minutes.

Add the pea and ham mixture, then stir in the parmesan. Serve immediately with the extra parmesan shavings, some freshly ground black pepper and a crunchy raw salad.

HINT:
• If fresh peas are in season, 500 g (1 lb 2 oz) peas in the pod will yield about 250 g (9 oz/1⅔ cups) shelled peas.

GREEN PEAS ARE A GOOD SOURCE OF
FOLATE AND FIBRE. THEIR SWEET
FLAVOUR AND BRIGHT COLOUR ALSO
MAKES THEM A HIT WITH CHILDREN.
THIS CARB-RICH DISH IS GOOD FOR
VERY ACTIVE KIDS.

nutrition per serve: Energy 1838 kJ (439 Cal)

Fat 13 g

Saturated fat 3.2 g

Protein 14.2 g

Carbohydrate 64 g

Fibre 3.4 g

Cholesterol 14 mg

# SALMON AND PASTA SALAD

THIS TASTY PASTA SALAD IS RICH IN THE LONG CHAIN OMEGA-3 FATS SO IMPORTANT FOR YOUR CHILDREN'S GROWTH AND DEVELOPMENT. IF YOU'RE SHORT ON TIME USE TINNED SALMON INSTEAD OF FRESH—YOU WON'T LOSE OUT ON THE NUTRITION.

500 g (1 lb 2 oz) salmon steaks
2 tbsp lemon juice
300 g (10½ oz) penne pasta
2 tbsp white wine vinegar
1 tbsp dijon mustard
3 tbsp olive oil
80 g (2¾ oz/½ cup) pine nuts, toasted
200 g (7 oz/heaped ¾ cup) ricotta cheese, crumbled
1 handful basil, roughly chopped
4 tbsp roughly chopped flat-leaf (Italian) parsley

35 g (1¼ oz/⅓ cup) coarsely grated parmesan cheese
1 large handful baby English spinach leaves
200 g (7 oz) cherry tomatoes, halved

PREP TIME: 20 MINUTES
COOKING TIME: 15 MINUTES
SERVES 4–6

Line a steamer with baking paper and punch small holes in the paper. Place the salmon on top and cover with a lid. Sit the steamer over a saucepan or wok of boiling water and steam for 5 minutes, or until just cooked (they should still be a little pink in the centre). Remove from the steamer. When the steaks are cool enough to handle, remove the skin and bones and break the flesh into chunks. Drizzle with lemon juice and season with salt and freshly ground black pepper.

Meanwhile, cook the pasta in a large saucepan of boiling water for 10 minutes, or until *al dente*. Drain and leave to cool.

To make a dressing, put the vinegar and mustard in a small jar and shake well. Add the oil and shake until combined. Set aside.

Put the salmon, penne, pine nuts, ricotta, basil, parsley, parmesan, spinach and tomatoes in a large bowl, drizzle with the dressing and toss gently to combine. Transfer to a large serving bowl.

nutrition per serve (6): Energy 2054 kJ (491 Cal); Fat 24.2 g; Saturated fat 5.9 g; Protein 30 g; Carbohydrate 36.3 g; Fibre 3.2 g; Cholesterol 65 mg

# FUSILLI WITH TUNA AND PARSLEY

WE ALL NEED TO GET INTO THE HABIT OF EATING FISH—BE IT FRESH OR TINNED—MORE OFTEN. THE COMBINATION OF TWO POPULAR FOODS, PASTA AND TUNA, MAKE THIS A NOURISHING MEAL THAT BOTH ADULTS AND CHILDREN WILL ENJOY.

**425 g (15 oz) tin tuna in spring water, drained**
**1 tbsp olive oil**
**1 garlic clove, finely chopped**
**2 roma (plum) tomatoes, diced**
**2 handfuls flat-leaf (Italian) parsley, chopped**

**3 tbsp lemon juice**
**375 g (13 oz) fusilli pasta**

PREP TIME: 10 MINUTES
COOKING TIME: 10 MINUTES
SERVES 4–6

Put the drained tuna in a bowl and flake lightly with a fork. In a small bowl, combine the oil, garlic, tomato, parsley and lemon juice. Pour over the tuna and mix lightly. Season with freshly ground black pepper.

Meanwhile, cook the pasta in a large saucepan of boiling water for 10 minutes, or until *al dente*. Just prior to draining the pasta, reserve 125 ml (4 fl oz/½ cup) of the pasta cooking water. Drain the pasta.

Toss the tuna mixture through the pasta, adding the reserved water from the pasta and serve immediately with a mixed leaf salad.

nutrition per serve (6): Energy 1284 kJ (307 Cal); Fat 5.1 g; Saturated fat 1 g; Protein 19.6 g; Carbohydrate 43.4 g; Fibre 2.6 g; Cholesterol 26 mg

ALL THE FLAVOURS OF THE
MEDITERRANEAN ARE IN THIS
TASTY VEGETARIAN DISH. THIS
LOW-GI MEAL ALSO PROVIDES
GOOD AMOUNTS OF ANTIOXIDANTS,
FIBRE, FOLATE AND POTASSIUM.

nutrition per serve (6): Energy 1279 kJ (306 Cal)
Fat 4.3 g
Saturated fat 0.7 g
Protein 9.7 g
Carbohydrate 53.6 g
Fibre 5.1 g
Cholesterol 0 mg

# TOMATO AND OLIVE PASTA

600 g (1 lb 5 oz) vine-ripened tomatoes,
   finely chopped
1 small red onion, finely chopped
2 garlic cloves, finely chopped
110 g (3¾ oz/½ cup) chopped pitted
   green olives
2 tbsp capers, rinsed and chopped
1 tsp dried oregano
1 tbsp olive oil
2 tsp white wine vinegar

400 g (14 oz) spaghetti
300 g (10½ oz) tin butter beans, drained
   and rinsed
1 handful oregano
grated parmesan cheese, to serve

PREP TIME: 15 MINUTES + 1 HOUR STANDING
COOKING TIME: 10 MINUTES
SERVES 4–6

Combine the tomato, onion, garlic, olives, capers and dried oregano in a bowl. Whisk together the olive oil and vinegar in a small bowl, then toss through the tomato mixture. Season to taste. Cover and set aside for at least 1 hour to allow the flavours to develop.

Meanwhile, cook the pasta in a large saucepan of boiling water for 10 minutes, or until *al dente*. Drain and return the pasta to the saucepan. Toss the tomato mixture and butter beans through the hot pasta. Divide among serving bowls and garnish with the oregano leaves. Serve with a lettuce salad.

# PENNE WITH PESTO, BEEF AND MUSHROOMS

THE SWEET RED AND YELLOW CAPSICUMS IN THIS DISH ARE MADE EVEN SWEETER WITH ROASTING. THEY ALSO ADD A VITAMIN BOOST DUE TO THEIR RICHNESS IN ANTIOXIDANT VITAMINS, BETA-CAROTENE AND VITAMIN C.

2 red capsicums (peppers)
1 yellow capsicum (pepper)
canola or olive oil spray
200 g (7 oz) lean beef fillet
150 g (5½ oz) button mushrooms,
    quartered
300 g (10½ oz) penne

125 g (4½ oz/½ cup) ready-made pesto
    or pesto (page 103)

PREP TIME: 20 MINUTES
COOKING TIME: 25 MINUTES
SERVES 4

Cut the capsicums into large flat pieces, removing the seeds and membrane. Put the capsicum pieces, skin side up, under a hot grill (broiler) until blackened. Leave covered with a tea towel (dish towel) until cool, then peel away the skin and chop the flesh.

Heat a frying pan over medium heat, spray with oil, then cook the steak over high heat for 3–4 minutes on each side. Remove and set aside for 5 minutes before chopping into bite-sized pieces or cut into very thin slices.

Spray the pan again, add the mushrooms and cook for 3–5 minutes, or until softened. Remove from the pan and set aside.

Cook the pasta in a large saucepan of boiling water for 10 minutes, or until *al dente*. Drain well and toss with the pesto in a large bowl. Add the capsicum, steak and mushrooms to the penne and toss to combine. Serve immediately with a mixed leaf salad.

nutrition per serve: Energy 2166 kJ (517 Cal); Fat 21 g; Saturated fat 4.1 g; Protein 24.2 g; Carbohydrate 54.9 g; Fibre 4 g; Cholesterol 33 mg

# RIGATONI WITH KIDNEY BEANS AND SAUSAGE

THIS RECIPE PROVES HOW EASY IT CAN BE TO INCLUDE LEGUMES IN YOUR DIET, AND SAUSAGES ARE ALWAYS A BIG HIT WITH CHILDREN. ANY LARGE PASTA SHAPE WILL WORK WELL IN THIS RECIPE.

2 tsp olive oil

1 large onion, chopped

2 garlic cloves, crushed

4 extra-lean beef sausages

2 x 400 g (14 oz) tins no-added-salt chopped tomatoes

400 g (14 oz) tin red kidney beans, drained and rinsed

2 tbsp chopped basil

1 tbsp chopped sage

1 tbsp chopped flat-leaf (Italian) parsley

500 g (1 lb 2 oz) rigatoni pasta

grated parmesan cheese, to serve (optional)

PREP TIME: 25 MINUTES

COOKING TIME: 35 MINUTES

SERVES 6–8

Heat the oil in a saucepan over medium heat. Add the onion, garlic and sausages and cook, stirring occasionally, for 5 minutes. Remove the sausages, chop them and return to the saucepan. Cook for 2 more minutes to brown.

Add the tomato, beans, basil, sage and parsley and season with freshly ground black pepper. Reduce the heat and simmer for 20 minutes.

Meanwhile, cook the pasta in a large saucepan of boiling water for 10 minutes, or until al dente. Drain well. Divide among serving bowls and top with the sauce. If you like, sprinkle with parmesan before serving.

HINTS:
- If you prefer, you can use dried beans instead of the tinned ones. Soak them overnight in water, then drain, transfer to a saucepan, cover with water and boil for 20 minutes, or until tender.
- Any leftovers can be frozen or stored in the refrigerator for up to 3 days.

nutrition per serve (8): Energy 1414 kJ (338 Cal); Fat 5.3 g; Saturated fat 1.4 g; Protein 15.2 g; Carbohydrate 53.7 g; Fibre 6.7 g; Cholesterol 4 mg

# MEATBALLS IN TOMATO SAUCE

500 g (1 lb 2 oz) lean minced (ground) beef

1 onion, very finely chopped

2 garlic cloves, finely chopped

1 egg, lightly beaten

80 g (2¾ oz/1 cup) fresh breadcrumbs

1 large handful flat-leaf (Italian) parsley, finely chopped

1 tbsp finely chopped oregano

canola or olive oil spray

700 ml (24 fl oz) bottle tomato passata (puréed tomatoes)

350 g (12 oz) penne pasta

chopped parsley, to garnish (optional)

PREP TIME: 20 MINUTES

COOKING TIME: 45 MINUTES

SERVES 6

Combine the beef, onion, garlic, egg, breadcrumbs, parsley and oregano in a large bowl. Season and mix well with your hands. Using about 1 tablespoon of beef mixture for each, shape into 36 small balls.

Spray a large, deep non-stick frying pan with oil. Cook a third of the meatballs over medium–high heat for 4–5 minutes, or until browned, turning constantly to prevent the meatballs sticking. Remove from the pan and repeat with the remaining meatballs.

Add the tomato passata to the pan along with the meatballs, then cover and simmer for another 15–20 minutes, or until the meatballs are just cooked.

Meanwhile, cook the pasta in a large saucepan of boiling water for 10 minutes, or until *al dente*. Drain well and serve with the meatballs and sauce. Garnish with some chopped parsley if desired, and serve with a side salad.

HINT:
• If you have a glut of tomatoes, you might prefer to substitute the bottle of passata with your own home-made tomato sauce (page 102)

SOMETHING A LITTLE DIFFERENT TO THE STANDARD SPAGHETTI BOLOGNAISE, THESE MEATBALLS WILL CERTAINLY ENSURE YOUR CHILDREN GET THEIR DAILY DOSE OF IRON.

nutrition per serve: Energy 1846 kJ (441 Cal)
Fat 9.2 g
Saturated fat 2.8 g
Protein 29.3 g
Carbohydrate 58.2 g
Fibre 5.5 g
Cholesterol 82 mg

**101**

# HOME-MADE TOMATO SAUCE

A BASIC TOMATO SAUCE IS AN ESSENTIAL STANDBY FOR BUSY FAMILIES, AND CAN BE MADE IN ADVANCE AND FROZEN IN PORTIONS. YOU CAN TOSS THE SAUCE THROUGH PASTA FOR A QUICK WEEKNIGHT MEAL, OR STIR IN SOME GRILLED TUNA, CHICKEN OR SLICED SAUSAGES AS WELL.

1.5 kg (3 lb 5 oz) ripe tomatoes
1 tbsp olive oil
2 onions, finely chopped
2 garlic cloves, finely chopped
125 g (4½ oz/½ cup) no-added-salt tomato paste (concentrated purée)
½ tsp sugar

1 handful flat-leaf (Italian) parsley, finely chopped
2 tbsp finely chopped oregano

PREP TIME: 20 MINUTES
COOKING TIME: 1 HOUR
MAKES ABOUT 1 KG (2 LB 4 OZ/4 CUPS)

Score a cross in the base of each tomato, place in a heatproof bowl and cover with boiling water. Leave for 1 minute, or until the skins start to come away. Drain, plunge into a bowl of iced water, then peel away the skin and roughly chop the flesh.

Heat the oil in a large, deep non-stick saucepan. Add the onion and garlic and cook over low heat for 2–3 minutes, stirring constantly. Add 2 tablespoons water, cover and cook gently for 5 minutes to soften the onion. Stir in the chopped tomatoes and tomato paste. Cover and simmer for 10 minutes, then uncover and simmer gently for 40 minutes. Add the sugar, parsley and oregano and season well.

Toss the sauce through pasta and serve with grated parmesan cheese, or use as a dipping sauce for sausage rolls or on pitta bread bases for pizzas.

HINT:
• Leftover tomato sauce can be stored in an airtight container in the refrigerator for up to 2 days, or in the freezer for up to 6 months.

nutrition per serve (½ cup): Energy 334 kJ (80 Cal); Fat 2.7 g; Saturated fat 0.3 g; Protein 2.5 g; Carbohydrate 9.3 g; Fibre 3.6 g; Cholesterol 0 mg

# PASTA PESTO

THIS IS A GOOD SAUCE TO HAVE READY IN THE FRIDGE FOR THE OCCASIONAL NIGHT WHEN YOU DON'T FEEL LIKE COOKING—ALL YOU'LL NEED TO DO IS BOIL THE PASTA. SERVE WITH A GREEN SALAD AND SOME RAW CARROT AND CELERY STICKS.

**500 g (1 lb 2 oz) pasta, such as linguine**
**3 tbsp pine nuts**
**85 g (3 oz/1 bunch) basil leaves**
**2 garlic cloves, peeled**
**3 tbsp grated parmesan cheese**
**2 tbsp grated pecorino cheese**
**100 ml (3½ fl oz) olive oil**

PREP TIME: 15 MINUTES
COOKING TIME: 15 MINUTES
SERVES 6

Cook the pasta in a large saucepan of boiling water for 10 minutes, or until *al dente*. Drain well and return the pasta to the pan to keep warm.

Meanwhile, toast the pine nuts in a frying pan over low heat for 2–3 minutes, or until golden. Set aside to cool.

Put the pine nuts, basil, garlic, ¼ teaspoon salt and cheeses in a food processor and process for 20 seconds, or until finely chopped. With the motor running, gradually add the oil in a thin steady stream until a paste is formed. Season to taste with freshly ground black pepper. Toss the pesto through the pasta until it is well coated and serve immediately.

HINTS:
• Pesto sauce can be stored in an airtight container in the refrigerator. Ensure the pesto is tightly packed in the container and seal the surface with some plastic wrap or pour a little extra oil over the top to prevent the pesto turning black. Each time you use some of the pesto, reseal the surface with a little more oil.
• While the fat is mostly the good kind, this meal is still higher in fat than most. If anyone in your family is watching their weight, enjoy it every now and then rather than having it on your regular weekly menu.

nutrition per serve: Energy 2076 kJ (496 Cal); Fat 23 g; Saturated fat 3.7 g; Protein 12.6 g; Carbohydrate 57.5 g; Fibre 3.9 g; Cholesterol 5 mg

THIS MEAL IS CONVENIENCE FOOD AT ITS NUTRITIOUS AND ITS BEST. IT'S ON THE TABLE IN ONLY 10 MINUTES, GIVING YOU JUST ENOUGH TIME TO PREPARE A SALAD OR A SELECTION OF RAW VEGETABLE STICKS TO SERVE IT UP WITH.

nutrition per serve: Energy 1807 kJ (432 Cal)
Fat 14.1 g
Saturated fat 4 g
Protein 24 g
Carbohydrate 51.1 g
Fibre 5.2 g
Cholesterol 29 mg

# GNOCCHI WITH TUNA AND CHEESE

**250 g (9 oz) ready-made potato gnocchi**
**125 g (4½ oz) tinned creamed corn**
**2 tbsp extra-light sour cream**
**95 g (3¼) tin tuna in spring water, drained**
**1–2 tbsp reduced-fat milk**
**40 g (1½ oz/⅓ cup) grated low-fat cheddar cheese**

PREP TIME: 10 MINUTES
COOKING TIME: 10 MINUTES
SERVES 2

Cook the gnocchi according to the directions on the packet, then drain and divide between two 310 ml (10¾ fl oz/1¼ cup) ramekins or heatproof dishes.

Combine the corn, sour cream and tuna in a small frying pan and stir over medium heat until hot. Add enough milk to the tuna mixture to reach the consistency of thickened cream. Pour the sauce evenly over the gnocchi, sprinkle with the cheese and place under a hot grill (broiler) and cook until the top is golden brown. Serve at once with a salad or vegetable sticks.

HINTS:
• For the best results, cook the gnocchi close to serving. If prepared too far ahead, the gnocchi will become chewy.
• For extra fibre, folate and antioxidants, add peas and parsley to this dish.

# SPINACH AND RICOTTA CANNELLONI

IF YOU HAVEN'T GOT TIME TO PREPARE THIS FROM SCRATCH, USING FROZEN
SPINACH WILL REDUCE THE COOKING AND PREPARATION TIME, MAKING IT
ACHIEVABLE ANY NIGHT OF THE WEEK.

20 g (¾ oz) margarine
1 onion, finely chopped
2 garlic cloves, crushed
900 g (2 lb/2 bunches) English spinach
300 g (10½ oz/1¼ cups) ricotta cheese
1 tbsp oregano
700 ml (24 fl oz) tomato passata (puréed
   tomatoes)
375 g (13 oz) fresh lasagne sheets
   (13 sheets)

50 g (1¾ oz/⅓ cup) grated mozzarella
   cheese
50 g (1¾ oz/½ cup) finely grated
   parmesan cheese

PREP TIME: 20 MINUTES
COOKING TIME: 40 MINUTES
SERVES 4–6

Preheat the oven to 180°C (350°F/Gas 4). Lightly grease a 2.5 litre (87 fl oz/10 cup)
ovenproof dish.

To make the filling, melt the margarine in a large frying pan, add the onion and garlic and
cook for 3–5 minutes, or until the onion softens. Wash the spinach well, trim and chop
the spinach, add it to the pan and cook for 5 minutes, or until wilted and the moisture
has evaporated. Remove from the heat. Once cooled, combine with the ricotta and
oregano in a food processor or blender. Process until smooth, then season with freshly
ground black pepper.

Spread one-third of the tomato passata over the base of the dish. Spoon 2 tablespoons
of the spinach mixture onto one lasagne sheet, spread it over the sheet, leaving a gap
along one long edge. Roll up the pasta and place, seam side down, in a row in the dish.
Repeat with all the lasagne, spacing the cannelloni evenly in the dish.

Spoon over the remaining tomato passata and sprinkle with the combined cheeses. Bake
for 30 minutes, or until the cheese is bubbling and golden. Stand for 5 minutes before
serving with a mixed salad.

nutrition per serve (6): Energy 1517 kJ (362 Cal); Fat 14.1 g; Saturated fat 7.1 g; Protein 21.3 g;
Carbohydrate 35.8 g; Fibre 8.9 g; Cholesterol 37 mg

# LASAGNE

THIS FAMILY FAVOURITE TAKES A LITTLE TIME TO PREPARE, BUT YOU'LL HAVE
LEFTOVERS FOR LUNCH THE NEXT DAY, OR PERHAPS ENOUGH FOR ANOTHER
MEAL, DEPENDING ON THE SIZE OF YOUR FAMILY.

2 tsp olive oil
1 large onion, chopped
2 carrots, finely chopped
2 celery stalks, finely chopped
2 zucchini (courgettes), finely chopped
2 garlic cloves, crushed
500 g (1 lb 2 oz) lean minced (ground) beef
2 x 400 g (14 oz) tins no-added-salt
   crushed tomatoes
125 ml (4 fl oz/½ cup) reduced-salt
   beef stock

2 tbsp no-added-salt tomato paste
   (concentrated purée)
2 tsp dried oregano
375 g (13 oz) dried or fresh lasagne sheets
750 ml (26 fl oz/3 cups) reduced-fat milk
40 g (1½ oz/⅓ cup) cornflour (cornstarch)
100 g (3½ oz) low-fat cheese, grated

PREP TIME: 40 MINUTES
COOKING TIME: 1 HOUR 35 MINUTES
SERVES 8

Heat the oil in a large non-stick frying pan and cook the onion for 5 minutes, or until soft.
Add the carrot, celery and zucchini and cook, stirring, for 5 minutes, or until the vegetables
are soft. Add the garlic and cook for another minute, then add the beef and cook over high
heat, stirring, until well browned. Break up any lumps of meat with a wooden spoon. Add
the crushed tomato, stock, tomato paste and oregano and stir to thoroughly combine.
Bring the mixture to the boil, then reduce the heat and simmer gently, partially covered,
for 20 minutes, stirring occasionally to prevent the mixture sticking to the pan.

Preheat the oven to 180°C (350°F/Gas 4).

Spread a little of the meat sauce into the base of a 23 x 30 cm (9 x 12 in) ovenproof dish.
Arrange a layer of lasagne sheets in the dish, breaking some of the sheets, if necessary,
to fit in neatly. Spread half the meat sauce over the top. Cover with another layer of
lasagne sheets, a layer of meat sauce, then a final layer of lasagne sheets.

To make the cheese sauce, blend a little of the milk with the cornflour in a small saucepan
to form a smooth paste. Gradually blend in the remaining milk and stir constantly over low
heat until the mixture boils and thickens. Remove from the heat and stir in the grated
cheese. Spread evenly over the top of the lasagne, then bake for 1 hour. Check the
lasagne after 25 minutes. If the top is browning too quickly, cover loosely with lightly oiled
foil. Leave the lasagne to stand for 15 minutes before serving. Serve with a green salad.

nutrition per serve: Energy 1532 kJ (366 Cal); Fat 8.7 g; Saturated fat 3.6 g; Protein 27.6 g;
Carbohydrate 42.5 g; Fibre 4.8 g; Cholesterol 43 mg

# MAIN MEALS

# NIÇOISE SALAD

3 eggs
60 ml (2 fl oz/¼ cup) olive oil
1 tbsp white wine vinegar
1 small garlic clove, crushed
300 g (10½ oz) iceberg lettuce, shredded
12 cherry tomatoes, cut into quarters
100 g (3½ oz) baby green beans, trimmed
   and blanched
1 small red capsicum (pepper), seeded
   and thinly sliced
1 celery stalk, cut into 5 cm (2 in) strips

1 Lebanese (short) cucumber, seeded,
   cut into 5 cm (2 in) strips
375 g (13 oz) tin tuna in spring water,
   drained and flaked
12 pitted kalamata olives, halved
4 anchovy fillets, finely chopped (optional)

PREP TIME: 20 MINUTES

COOKING TIME: 10 MINUTES

SERVES 4

Put the eggs in a saucepan of cold water. Bring slowly to the boil, then reduce the heat and simmer for 10 minutes. Stir the water during the first few minutes to centre the yolk. Drain and cool under cold water, then peel and cut into quarters.

Combine the oil, vinegar and garlic in a small bowl and mix well. Put the lettuce, tomato, beans, capsicum, celery, cucumber, tuna, olives and anchovies in a large bowl. Pour over the dressing and toss well to combine. Top the salad with the egg quarters and serve with some crusty wholegrain bread.

HINT:
• Use omega-3-enriched eggs to increase the proportion of healthy omega-3 fat in
  this dish.

TINNED TUNA IS A TASTY NUTRITIOUS
FOOD AND A GOOD SOURCE OF THE
OMEGA-3 FATS THAT ARE SUCH GOOD
BRAIN FOOD FOR GROWING CHILDREN.
THIS SALAD IS A GREAT WAY TO
INCLUDE A VARIETY OF HEALTHY
FOODS IN YOUR CHILD'S DIET.

nutrition per serve: Energy 1310 kJ (313 Cal)
Fat 20.1 g
Saturated fat 3.9 g
Protein 24.5 g
Carbohydrate 6.7 g
Fibre 3.7 g
Cholesterol 199 mg

# GADO GADO

RICH IN PROTEIN FROM THE EGGS, BETA-CAROTENE FROM THE CARROTS AND SWEET POTATO, AND VITAMIN C FROM THE CABBAGE, GADO GADO IS A NUTRITIOUS SALAD-STYLE MEAL THAT CHILDREN WILL LOVE.

**PEANUT SAUCE**

1 tbsp canola oil

1 small onion, finely chopped

125 g (4$\frac{1}{2}$ oz/$\frac{1}{2}$ cup) reduced-fat smooth peanut butter

185 ml (6 fl oz/$\frac{3}{4}$ cup) light coconut milk

1 tbsp lemon juice

1 tbsp reduced-salt dark soy sauce

**SALAD**

3 eggs

2 orange sweet potatoes, cut into 1 cm ($\frac{1}{2}$ in) thick slices

2 potatoes, halved and cut into 1 cm ($\frac{1}{2}$ in) thick slices

125 g (4$\frac{1}{2}$ oz) baby (pattypan) squash, halved

2 carrots, cut into 1 cm ($\frac{1}{2}$ in) thick strips

250 g (9 oz) cabbage, cut into wedges

1 cucumber

125 g (4$\frac{1}{2}$ oz/1$\frac{1}{3}$ cups) bean sprouts

PREP TIME: 20 MINUTES

COOKING TIME: 35 MINUTES

SERVES 6

To make the peanut sauce, heat the oil in a saucepan over low heat, add the onion and cook for 5 minutes, or until soft and lightly golden. Add the peanut butter, coconut milk, lemon juice, soy sauce and 3 tablespoons water and stir well. Bring to the boil, stirring constantly, then reduce the heat and simmer for 5 minutes, or until the sauce has reduced and thickened.

To make the salad, put the eggs in a saucepan with cold water to cover. Bring to the boil, reduce to a simmer and cook for 10 minutes; stir the water during the first few minutes to centre the yolk. Drain and cool under cold water.

Bring a large saucepan of water to the boil. Blanch each type of vegetable separately in the boiling water; they must be firm and not overcooked. The sweet potato and potato will each need 8–10 minutes; the squash 1 minute; the carrots 2 minutes; and the cabbage 2 minutes. Remove the vegetables from the water with a slotted spoon and plunge into a bowl of iced water to stop the cooking process and set the colour.

Drain the vegetables and dry briefly on paper towels. Shell the boiled eggs and cut into quarters. Slice the cucumber into thin strips. Arrange the vegetables in groups and garnish with the sliced eggs and bean sprouts. Top with the peanut sauce. Serve with rice noodles.

nutrition per serve: Energy 1301 kJ (311 Cal); Fat 15.6 g; Saturated fat 4.1 g; Protein 11.8 g; Carbohydrate 28.2 g; Fibre 6.5 g; Cholesterol 107 mg

# TUNA AND BEAN SALAD

HEALTHY, FILLING AND TASTY, THIS SALAD PROVIDES PROTEIN, LOW-GI
CARBOHYDRATE AND FIBRE. IT ALSO CONTAINS ANTIOXIDANTS SUCH AS
VITAMIN C, BETA-CAROTENE AND FLAVONOIDS.

**100 g (3½ oz) green beans, trimmed
and chopped**
**400 g (14 oz) tin butter beans, drained
and rinsed**
**425 g (15 oz) tin tuna in spring water,
drained**
**200 g (7 oz) cherry tomatoes, halved**
**1 small red onion, thinly sliced**
**200 g (7 oz) mixed salad leaves**

**DRESSING**
**2 tsp olive oil**
**3 tbsp lemon juice**
**1 tsp honey**
**1 garlic clove, crushed**
**2 tbsp chopped dill**

PREP TIME: 20 MINUTES + 10 MINUTES
   REFRIGERATION
COOKING TIME: 5 MINUTES
SERVES 4

Steam the green beans until tender, then rinse under cold water and drain well. Put the
green beans, butter beans, tuna, tomato and onion in a bowl and toss well.

To make the dressing, whisk all the ingredients together. Pour over the tuna mixture, cover
and refrigerate for 10 minutes. Arrange the salad leaves on a platter. Top with the tuna
mixture and serve with crusty wholegrain bread.

nutrition per serve: Energy 692 kJ (165 Cal); Fat 4.6 g; Saturated fat 1.1 g; Protein 21.7 g;
Carbohydrate 6.6 g; Fibre 4 g; Cholesterol 39 mg

WITH NO STOVETOP COOKING, THIS RECIPE IS A GREAT ONE FOR KIDS TO MAKE THEMSELVES. AND, LETTING THEM BE INVOLVED IN MEALTIME PREPARATIONS HELPS THEM GAIN A BETTER UNDERSTANDING OF HEALTHY FOOD CHOICES.

nutrition per roll: Energy 502 kJ (120 Cal)
Fat 2.3 g
Saturated fat 0.6 g
Protein 7.6 g
Carbohydrate 16.9 g
Fibre 0.4 g
Cholesterol 25 mg

# FRESH SPRING ROLLS

½ **barbecued chicken (see Hints)**
**50 g (1¾ oz) dried mung bean vermicelli**
**8 x 17 cm (6½ in) square dried rice paper**
  **wrappers**
**16 Thai basil leaves**
**1 large handful coriander (cilantro) leaves**
**1 carrot, cut into short thin strips, blanched**
**2 tbsp plum sauce**

PREP TIME: 30 MINUTES
COOKING TIME: NIL
MAKES 8

Remove the meat from the chicken bones, discard the skin and finely shred the meat. Soak the vermicelli in hot water for 10 minutes, drain and transfer to a bowl.

Working with one rice paper wrapper at a time, dip it into a bowl of warm water until it softens, then place it on a clean work surface. Put one-eighth of the chicken in the centre of the wrapper and top with two basil leaves, a few coriander leaves, a few carrot strips and a small amount of vermicelli. Spoon a little plum sauce over the top.

Press the filling down to flatten it a little, then fold in the two sides and roll it up tightly like a parcel. Lay the roll, seam side down, on a serving plate and sprinkle with a little water. Cover with a damp tea towel (dish towel) and repeat the process with the remaining ingredients. Serve with your favourite dipping sauce or a little extra plum sauce.

HINTS:
• When buying the barbecued chicken, ask for two breast quarters.
• Rice paper wrappers must be kept moist or they become brittle. If you leave the rolls for any length of time and they start to dry out, sprinkle cold water on them.

**115**

# PITTA PIZZAS

PIZZAS ARE POPULAR WITH CHILDREN, BUT THE COMMERCIAL VARIETIES ARE OFTEN HIGH IN FAT. THE MEDITERRANEAN-STYLE TOPPING BELOW IS ONE OPTION, AND WE'VE LISTED SOME OTHER IDEAS AT THE END OF THE RECIPE.

4 large wholemeal (whole-wheat) pitta pocket breads
130 g (4½ oz/½ cup) ready-made tomato salsa
½ red onion, thinly sliced
90 g (3¼ oz) mushrooms, thinly sliced
60 g (2¼ oz) low-fat ham, thinly sliced
90 g (3¼ oz/¾ cup) pitted black olives in brine, rinsed and chopped

80 g (2¾ oz/½ cup) crumbled reduced-fat feta cheese
1 handful rosemary sprigs
75 g (2½ oz/½ cup) grated reduced-fat mozzarella cheese

PREP TIME: 15 MINUTES
COOKING TIME: 20 MINUTES
MAKES 4

Preheat the oven to 200°C (400°F/Gas 6). Place the pitta breads on a large baking tray. Spread each pitta with the salsa. Scatter over the onion, mushrooms, ham and olives.

Crumble over the feta and top with the rosemary and mozzarella. Bake for 20 minutes, or until the base is crispy and the cheese has melted. Serve with a salad.

HINT:
• If preferred, use smaller-sized pitta breads for younger children.

VARIATIONS:
• Use home-made tomato sauce (see recipe, page 102) or salsa sauce on the base, then choose from the following toppings: ham, pineapple pieces, sliced capsicum (pepper), onion or olives marinated in brine.
• For a meaty topping, try leftover spaghetti bolognaise and low-fat cheddar cheese.
For a little spice, try salami, corn kernels, sliced green capsicum (pepper), onion, tomato and low-fat feta cheese.
• A tasty vegetarian option is artichoke hearts, tomato and zucchini (courgette) slices, topped with ricotta and low-fat feta cheeses.
• For an easy seafood version, use tuna in spring water, sliced mushroom and capsicum (pepper), and low-fat cheddar cheese.

nutrition per pizza: Energy 1755 kJ (419 Cal); Fat 8.6 g; Saturated fat 4.1 g; Protein 23.1 g; Carbohydrate 59 g; Fibre 8.5 g; Cholesterol 24 mg

# BATTERED FISH AND CHUNKY WEDGES

EVERYONE ENJOYS FRIED FISH AND CHIPS BUT BECAUSE IT IS HIGHER IN FAT IT'S BEST KEPT AS A SPECIAL TREAT MEAL. COOKED WITH HEALTHY FATS AND TAKING CARE TO DRAIN IT WELL, THIS MEAL IS A FUN WAY TO GET CHILDREN EATING FISH.

**3 all-purpose potatoes**
**oil, for deep-frying**
**125 g (4½ oz/1 cup) self-raising flour**
**1 egg, beaten**
**185 ml (6 fl oz/¾ cup) reduced-fat milk**
**4 firm white fish fillets**

**plain (all-purpose) flour, for dusting**
**lemon wedges, to serve**

PREP TIME: 15 MINUTES
COOKING TIME: 15 MINUTES
SERVES 4

Wash the potatoes well, but do not peel them. Cut into thick wedges, then dry with paper towels. Fill a large heavy-based saucepan two-thirds full with oil and heat. Gently lower the potato wedges into medium–hot oil. Cook for 4 minutes, or until tender and lightly browned. Carefully remove the wedges from the oil with a slotted spoon and drain on paper towels.

Sift the self-raising flour with some freshly ground black pepper into a large bowl and make a well in the centre. Add the combined egg and milk. Using a wooden spoon, stir until just combined and smooth. The consistency should be of thick cream. Thin with a little extra milk if necessary. Dust the fish fillets in the plain flour, shaking off the excess. Add the fish fillets one at a time to the batter and turn to coat in the batter. Remove from the batter, draining off the excess.

Working with one piece of fish at a time, gently lower it into the medium–hot oil. Cook for 2 minutes, or until golden and crisp and cooked through. Carefully remove from the oil with a slotted spoon. Drain on paper towels and keep warm while you cook the remainder.

Return the potato wedges to the medium–hot oil. Cook for another 2 minutes, or until golden brown and crisp. Remove from the oil with a slotted spoon and drain on paper towels. Serve the wedges immediately with the fish and lemon wedges. Serve with your child's favourite dipping sauce.

nutrition per serve: Energy 1996 kJ (477 Cal); Fat 12.5 g; Saturated fat 2.8 g; Protein 41.7 g; Carbohydrate 46.3 g; Fibre 4.1 g; Cholesterol 140 mg

# SAN CHOY BAU

4 dried Chinese mushrooms

1 tbsp reduced-salt soy sauce

1 tbsp lime juice

1 tsp sesame oil

4 tbsp chopped coriander (cilantro) leaves

2 tbsp chopped mint

1 tbsp vegetable oil

30 g (1 oz/¼ cup) slivered almonds, chopped

125 g (4½ oz) water chestnuts, drained and finely chopped

1 carrot, finely chopped

4 spring onions (scallions), finely chopped

250 g (9 oz) lean minced (ground) pork

4 coriander (cilantro) roots, finely chopped

1 tbsp grated fresh ginger

12 lettuce leaves

hoisin sauce, to serve

PREP TIME: 25 MINUTES + 10 MINUTES SOAKING

COOKING TIME: 10 MINUTES

SERVES 4

Soak the mushrooms in a small bowl of hot water for 10 minutes, or until softened. Discard the stems and finely chop the mushroom caps.

Combine the soy sauce, lime juice, sesame oil, coriander leaves and mint in a small bowl. Set aside.

Heat the wok until very hot, add half the oil and swirl it around to coat the base and side of the wok. Add the almonds, water chestnuts, carrot and spring onion to the wok and stir-fry for 1 minute, or until lightly cooked but not browned—they should still be crisp. Remove from the wok and set aside.

Reheat the wok with the remaining vegetable oil, add the pork, coriander root, ginger and mushrooms and stir-fry over medium–high heat for 2–3 minutes, or until the pork changes colour; do not overcook the pork or it will be tough.

Add the soy sauce and lime mixture and stir to combine. Return the vegetable mixture to the wok and stir-fry for 1–2 minutes, or until heated through and the mixture is well combined. Spoon the pork into the lettuce leaves and wrap up to eat. Serve with hoisin sauce for dipping.

PLACE THE PREPARED PORK, LETTUCE AND HOISIN SAUCE IN BOWLS ON THE TABLE AND LET EVERYONE ASSEMBLE THEIR OWN. IT CAN GET A BIT MESSY BUT MAKES FOR A GREAT INTERACTIVE MEAL. SERVE WITH STEAMED RICE TO PROVIDE SOME CARBOHYDRATE TO MAKE THE MEAL COMPLETE.

nutrition per serve: Energy 1134 kJ (271 Cal)
Fat 15 g
Saturated fat 2.1 g
Protein 17.9 g
Carbohydrate 14 g
Fibre 4.6 g
Cholesterol 19 mg

# VEAL SCHNITZEL

SERVE THIS QUICK, IRON-RICH MEAL WITH YOUR CHILD'S FAVOURITE VEGETABLES,
A GREEN SALAD OR ONE OF THE SIDE DISHES LISTED ON PAGES 139–142.

**4 thin veal steaks**
**100 g (3½ oz/1 cup) dry breadcrumbs**
**½ tsp dried basil**
**25 g (1 oz/¼ cup) grated parmesan cheese**
**1 egg, lightly beaten**
**1 tbsp milk**
**plain (all-purpose) flour, for coating**
**oil, for frying**

PREP TIME: 20 MINUTES + CHILLING
COOKING TIME: 5 MINUTES
SERVES 4

Trim the meat of any excess fat. Place the veal between sheets of plastic wrap and flatten with a meat mallet or rolling pin until 3 mm (⅛ in) thick. Nick the edges of the meat with a knife to prevent curling.

Combine the breadcrumbs, basil and parmesan on a sheet of baking paper. Combine the egg and milk in a wide bowl.

Coat the veal in the flour, shaking off the excess. Working with one at a time, dip the veal steak into the egg mixture, then coat with the breadcrumb mixture. Lightly shake off the excess. Refrigerate for 30 minutes to firm the coating.

Heat the oil in a large frying pan and cook the veal over medium heat for 2–3 minutes on each side, or until golden and cooked through. Drain on paper towels and serve.

nutrition per serve: Energy 1587 kJ (379 Cal); Fat 14.7 g; Saturated fat 3.8 g; Protein 38 g; Carbohydrate 22.8 g; Fibre 1.4 g; Cholesterol 166 mg

# TOFU AND VEGETABLE KOFTAS

TOFU IS RICH IN GOOD QUALITY PROTEIN NECESSARY FOR GROWING BODIES.
BALANCE OUT THE NUTRITION AND COLOUR OF THIS MEAL BY SERVING IT
WITH A GREEN SALAD OR A SELECTION OF COOKED GREEN VEGETABLES.

250 g (9 oz) firm tofu
1 tbsp olive oil
185 g (6$\frac{1}{2}$ oz/1$\frac{1}{2}$ cups) grated pumpkin
   (winter squash)
100 g (3$\frac{1}{2}$ oz/$\frac{3}{4}$ cup) grated zucchini
   (courgette)
1 onion, chopped
2 garlic cloves, crushed
4 small spring onions (scallions), chopped
1 handful coriander (cilantro) leaves,
   chopped
1 tbsp mild curry powder
150 g (5$\frac{1}{2}$ oz/1 cup) wholemeal
   (whole-wheat) flour

50 g (1$\frac{3}{4}$ oz/$\frac{1}{2}$ cup) grated parmesan
   cheese
oil, for deep-frying

YOGHURT DIPPING SAUCE
200 g (7 oz) low-fat plain yoghurt
1 garlic clove, crushed
2 tbsp finely chopped mint

PREP TIME: 25 MINUTES
COOKING TIME: 20 MINUTES
SERVES 4–6

To make the yoghurt dipping sauce, put the yoghurt, garlic and mint in a small bowl and mix together well. Add a little water, if needed. Set aside.

Blend the tofu in a food processor or blender until finely processed.

Heat the oil in a frying pan. Add the pumpkin, zucchini, onion and garlic and cook over low–medium heat, stirring occasionally, for 10 minutes, or until the vegetables are tender. Remove to a bowl and leave to cool.

Add the spring onion, coriander, curry powder, 75 g (2$\frac{1}{2}$ oz/$\frac{1}{2}$ cup) of the wholemeal flour, the parmesan, tofu and a pinch of salt to the vegetables and mix well. Roll a tablespoon of the mixture between your hands to form a ball, then repeat with the remaining mixture to make about 36 balls. Coat the balls in the remaining flour.

Fill a deep heavy-based saucepan one-third full of oil and heat to 180°C (350°F), or until a cube of bread browns in 15 seconds. Cook the koftas in small batches for 2–3 minutes, or until golden brown. Drain on paper towels. Serve the koftas with the yoghurt dipping sauce, and rice or naan bread.

nutrition per serve (6): Energy 1188 kJ (284 Cal); Fat 14.2 g; Saturated fat 3.4 g; Protein 14.6 g; Carbohydrate 21.8 g; Fibre 5.2 g; Cholesterol 10 mg

MAKE THIS AN INTERACTIVE MEAL
FOR CHILDREN TO ASSEMBLE
THEMSELVES. THIS DISH IS
A GOOD SOURCE OF FIBRE AND
PROVIDES GOOD AMOUNTS OF
FOLATE AND ANTIOXIDANTS.

nutrition per enchilada: Energy 924 kJ (221 Cal)
Fat 9.7 g
Saturated fat 1.8 g
Protein 8.1 g
Carbohydrate 22.4 g
Fibre 6.6 g
Cholesterol 0.3 mg

# BEAN ENCHILADAS

3 tomatoes
1 tbsp light olive oil
1 onion, thinly sliced
3 garlic cloves, crushed
2 tsp ground cumin
125 ml (4 fl oz/½ cup) reduced-salt
   vegetable stock
1 tbsp no-added-salt tomato paste
   (concentrated purée)
2 x 420 g (15 oz) tins three-bean mix
2 tbsp chopped coriander (cilantro) leaves

8 flour tortillas
1 avocado, chopped
2 tbsp low-fat plain yoghurt
1 handful coriander (cilantro) sprigs
115 g (4 oz/2 cups) shredded lettuce

PREP TIME: 20 MINUTES
COOKING TIME: 25 MINUTES
MAKES 8

Preheat the oven to 170°C (325°F/Gas 3).

To peel the tomatoes, score a cross in the base of each tomato, place in a heatproof bowl and cover with boiling water. Leave for 1 minute, or until the skins start to come away. Drain, plunge into a bowl of iced water, then peel away the skin, cut in half and scoop out the seeds and then roughly chop the flesh.

Heat the oil in a deep frying pan over medium heat. Add the onion and cook for 4 minutes, or until just soft. Add the garlic and cook for a further 30 seconds. Add the cumin, stock, tomato and tomato paste and cook for 6–8 minutes, or until the mixture is quite thick and pulpy. Season with freshly ground black pepper.

Drain and rinse the bean mix. Add the beans to the sauce and cook for 5 minutes to heat through, then add the chopped coriander leaves.

Meanwhile, wrap the tortillas in foil and warm in the oven for 3–4 minutes. Put the avocado and yoghurt in a bowl and mash it with a fork to combine.

Place a tortilla on a plate and spread with a large scoop of the bean mixture. Top with some avocado and yoghurt mixture, coriander sprigs and lettuce. Roll the enchiladas up, tucking in the ends. Cut each one in half to serve.

HINTS:
- For beef enchiladas, use only half the quantity of three-bean mix and add 500 g (1 lb 2 oz) lean minced (ground) beef. Cook the beef with the garlic for 5–6 minutes, or until browned and cooked through, breaking up any lumps with the back of a spoon.
- You can use extra-light sour cream instead of the yoghurt if preferred.

# HOKKIEN NOODLE AND BEEF STIR-FRY

THE WHOLE FAMILY WILL ENJOY THIS STIR-FRY, WHICH INCLUDES A VARIETY OF COLOURFUL VEGETABLES. HOKKIEN NOODLES ARE THICK, FRESH NOODLES MADE FROM EGG AND WHEAT, AND THEIR LONG LENGTHS ARE ALWAYS POPULAR WITH CHILDREN.

600 g (1 lb 5 oz) hokkien (egg) noodles
canola or olive oil spray
350 g (12 oz) lean beef fillet, partially frozen, thinly sliced
1 tbsp peanut oil
1 large onion, cut into thin wedges
1 large carrot, thinly sliced on the diagonal
1 red capsicum (pepper), cut into thin strips
4 spears fresh baby corn, sliced on the diagonal
2 garlic cloves, crushed

1 tsp grated fresh ginger
100 g (3½ oz) snow peas (mangetout), sliced in half on the diagonal
3 tbsp oyster sauce
2 tbsp reduced-salt soy sauce
1 tbsp soft brown sugar
½ tsp Chinese five-spice

PREP TIME: 15 MINUTES
COOKING TIME: 15 MINUTES
SERVES 4

Put the noodles in a heatproof bowl with enough boiling water to cover. Leave to soften for 1 minute, separate the noodles with a fork, then drain and set aside.

Spray a large wok with oil and heat over high heat. Add the beef in batches and cook until brown. Remove and keep warm.

Heat the peanut oil in the wok, and when very hot, add the onion, carrot, capsicum and corn and stir-fry for 2–3 minutes, or until tender. Add the garlic, ginger and snow peas and cook for another minute, then return the beef to the wok.

Add the noodles to the wok, tossing well. Combine the oyster sauce with the soy sauce, sugar, five-spice powder and 1 tablespoon water and pour over the noodles. Toss until warmed through and serve immediately.

nutrition per serve: Energy 1775 kJ (424 Cal); Fat 11.7 g; Saturated fat 3.2 g; Protein 26.9 g; Carbohydrate 50.3 g; Fibre 5.5 g; Cholesterol 59 mg

# TANDOORI CHICKEN

SERVE THIS TASTY CHICKEN WITH THE CUCUMBER RAITA AND NAAN BREAD ON THE SIDE, OR ALTERNATIVELY USE MOUNTAIN BREAD AND FILL IT WITH SLICED CHICKEN, TOPPED WITH THE RAITA AND SOME SALAD. ROLL IT UP AND IT'S READY TO EAT.

125 g (4½ oz/½ cup) low-fat Greek-style
   yoghurt
2 tbsp tandoori paste
2 garlic cloves, crushed
2 tbsp lime juice
1½ tsp garam masala
2 tbsp finely chopped coriander (cilantro)
   leaves
6 boneless, skinless chicken thighs,
   trimmed of fat

**CUCUMBER RAITA**
1 Lebanese (short) cucumber, coarsely
   grated
200 g (7 oz) low-fat Greek-style yoghurt
1 tbsp chopped mint
2 tsp lemon juice

PREP TIME: 15 MINUTES + 1 HOUR
  MARINATING
COOKING TIME: 15 MINUTES
SERVES 4

Combine the yoghurt, tandoori paste, garlic, lime juice, garam masala and coriander in a bowl and mix well.

Add the chicken, coat well, then cover and refrigerate for at least 1 hour.

Meanwhile, to make the cucumber raita, put the cucumber in a bowl, add the yoghurt, mint and lemon juice and stir well until combined. Refrigerate until needed.

Preheat a barbecue or chargrill plate and lightly brush with oil. Cook the chicken, in batches if necessary, for 10–15 minutes over medium heat, turning once, and basting with the remaining marinade until golden and cooked through. Serve with the cucumber raita and naan bread or rice.

nutrition per serve: Energy 1778 kJ (425 Cal); Fat 19 g; Saturated fat 5.7 g; Protein 53.2 g; Carbohydrate 9 g; Fibre 1 g; Cholesterol 226 mg

# CHICKEN SATAY

1 tbsp mild curry powder
1 tbsp fish sauce
1 tbsp shaved palm sugar (jaggery) or soft
  brown sugar
2 garlic cloves, crushed
80 ml (2½ fl oz/⅓ cup) oil
12 chicken tenderloins
1 small handful coriander (cilantro) leaves

2 tbsp fried shallots (see Hint)
peanut sauce (page 112), warmed,
  to serve

PREP TIME: 20 MINUTES + 3 HOURS
  MARINATING
COOKING TIME: 5 MINUTES
MAKES 12 SKEWERS

Soak 12 bamboo skewers in water to prevent scorching. To make the marinade, combine the curry powder, fish sauce, palm sugar, garlic and oil in a bowl.

Thread each chicken tenderloin onto a bamboo skewer and place in a shallow ceramic or glass dish. Pour the marinade over the skewers, turning to coat the chicken. Cover and chill for 3 hours, or overnight.

Preheat the barbecue or a chargrill pan to high. Cook the chicken skewers, turning several times, for 5 minutes, or until cooked through. Arrange the chicken skewers on a plate, sprinkle with the coriander and fried shallots and serve with a bowl of the warm satay sauce, for dipping. Serve with rice and steamed vegetables.

HINT:
• Crunchy fried shallots are available from Asian grocery stores and larger supermarkets.

KIDS LOVE MEALS THAT DON'T
INVOLVE A KNIFE AND A FORK.
BOOST THEIR DAILY FIBRE
INTAKE BY SERVING THE SATAYS
ON A BED OF BROWN RICE WITH
STEAMED GREEN BEANS AND
BROCCOLI, GREAT FOR DIPPING
IN ANY EXTRA SATAY SAUCE.

nutrition per skewer: Energy 681 kJ (163 Cal)
Fat 7.2 g
Saturated fat 1.3 g
Protein 22.2 g
Carbohydrate 2.1 g
Fibre 0.3 g
Cholesterol 80 mg

# FISH PARCELS WITH SOY AND VEGIE STRIPS

FULL OF THE GOOD FATS IMPORTANT FOR BRAIN DEVELOPMENT, FISH SHOULD BE A WEEKLY PART OF THE FAMILY MENU, AND THE KIDS WILL LOVE HAVING THEIR OWN INDIVIDUAL FOOD PARCELS TO OPEN UP AT THE TABLE.

**2 x 150 g (5½ oz) pieces boneless firm white fish fillets**
**½ carrot, cut into long, thin matchsticks**
**½ celery stalk, cut into long, thin matchsticks**
**2 tsp reduced-salt soy sauce**
**½ tsp sesame oil**

PREP TIME: 5 MINUTES
COOKING TIME: 15–20 MINUTES
SERVES 2

Preheat the oven to 180°C (350°F/Gas 4). Place each piece of fish onto a lightly greased sheet of baking paper, large enough to enclose the fish.

Place the carrot and celery strips on top of the fish and drizzle with the soy sauce and sesame oil. Wrap the paper around the fish to enclose and tuck the ends under to seal. Place the parcels on a baking tray and bake for 15–20 minutes, or until the fish is cooked through and flakes easily when tested with a fork.

Serve the fish in the parcel, with noodles or steamed rice and stir-fried vegetables such as broccolini and snow peas (mangetout).

nutrition per serve: Energy 736 kJ (176 Cal); Fat 5.4 g; Saturated fat 1.6 g; Protein 29.9 g; Carbohydrate 1.2 g; Fibre 0.6 g; Cholesterol 90 mg

# THAI CHICKEN BURGERS

THESE EASTERN-STYLE BURGERS ARE DELICIOUSLY DIFFERENT FROM
COMMERCIAL BURGERS. THEY ALSO HAVE LESS FAT AND MORE NUTRIENTS.
THIS RECIPE MAKES FOUR PATTIES, BUT FOR YOUNGER CHILDREN YOU MIGHT
LIKE TO MAKE SMALLER PATTIES AND USE SMALL BUNS OR TOAST.

400 g (14 oz) lean minced (ground) chicken
80 g (2¾ oz/1 cup) fresh breadcrumbs
1 garlic clove, crushed
1 large handful coriander (cilantro) leaves,
  chopped, plus 1 tbsp, extra
3 tbsp sweet chilli sauce
1 tsp ground coriander
3 spring onions (scallions), finely chopped
60 g (2¼ oz/¼ cup) sugar
2 tbsp white vinegar
2 tbsp finely chopped raw or dry-roasted
  peanuts

canola or olive oil spray
4 hamburger or wholegrain buns
2 handfuls mixed lettuce leaves
1 vine-ripened tomato, sliced
1 carrot, peeled into thin ribbons
1 Lebanese (short) cucumber, peeled
  into thin ribbons

PREP TIME: 25 MINUTES + 30 MINUTES
  REFRIGERATION
COOKING TIME: 15 MINUTES
SERVES 4

Put the chicken, breadcrumbs, garlic, fresh coriander, chilli sauce, ground coriander and
spring onion in a large bowl and mix together with your hands. Shape into four patties.
Refrigerate, covered, for 30 minutes.

To make the dressing, put the sugar, vinegar and 3 tablespoons water in a small saucepan
and stir over low heat until the sugar dissolves. Simmer for 5 minutes, or until slightly
thickened. Cool and stir in the peanuts and extra coriander.

Heat a chargrill plate or barbecue, spray with the oil and cook the burgers for 4 minutes
on each side, or until tender. Serve the patties on the hamburger buns, drizzle with the
dressing and top with the lettuce, tomato, carrot and cucumber.

HINT:
• To save time in the evening, make a batch of the chicken patties on the weekend and
  freeze them individually. Pull them out when you are ready to eat them. They will freeze
  for 1 month.

nutrition per serve: Energy 2527 kJ (604 Cal); Fat 15.3 g; Saturated fat 3.6 g; Protein 32.9 g;
Carbohydrate 77.7 g; Fibre 5.7 g; Cholesterol 90 mg

THIS TASTY, TENDER MEAL, RICH IN
IRON AND ZINC, WILL TEMPT EVEN
THE MOST RELUCTANT OF MEAT
EATERS. SERVE WITH MASHED
POTATO, STEAMED RICE, POLENTA
OR COUSCOUS AND A SELECTION OF
COOKED WINTER VEGETABLES.

nutrition per serve: Energy 1257 kJ (300 Cal)
Fat 13.7 g
Saturated fat 2.8 g
Protein 33 g
Carbohydrate 8.6 g
Fibre 1.7 g
Cholesterol 105 mg

# OSSO BUCCO

8 large veal shanks, sliced
plain (all-purpose) flour, for dusting
3 tbsp oil
1 onion, finely chopped
1 carrot, finely diced
1 celery stalk, finely diced
1 bay leaf
2 garlic cloves, crushed

1.25 litres (44 fl oz/5 cups) reduced-salt
  beef stock
400 g (14 oz) tin no-added-salt diced
  tomatoes

PREP TIME: 20 MINUTES
COOKING TIME: 2 HOURS 50 MINUTES
SERVES 6

Lightly dust the veal shanks in flour, shaking off the excess. Heat 2 tablespoons of the oil in a casserole dish or large heavy-based saucepan over high heat. Add the veal and cook in two batches for 2–3 minutes on each side, or until golden. Remove from the dish.

Reduce the heat to low and add the remaining oil to the dish. When the oil is hot, add the onion, carrot, celery and bay leaf and cook for about 10 minutes, or until the vegetables are softened and golden.

Add the garlic, stock and tomato and then return the veal to the dish. Bring to the boil, then reduce the heat and simmer for 2½ hours, or until the meat is very tender. Serve with mashed potato and winter vegetables.

HINT:
• This recipe works with other less expensive cuts such as lamb forequarter pieces.

# SHEPHERD'S PIE

THIS HEARTY DISH COMBINES TWO CHILDREN'S FAVOURITES: MINCED MEAT AND MASHED POTATO. IF YOU HAVE ENOUGH RAMEKINS YOU COULD ALSO MAKE THEM INDIVIDUALLY, WHICH WILL MEAN THEY'RE AN EVEN BIGGER HIT.

canola or olive oil spray
2 onions, thinly sliced
1 large carrot, finely chopped
2 celery stalks, finely chopped
500 g (1 lb 2 oz) lean minced (ground) lamb
2 tbsp plain (all-purpose) flour
2 tbsp no-added-salt tomato paste (concentrated purée)
2 tbsp worcestershire sauce

500 ml (17 fl oz/2 cups) reduced-salt beef or chicken stock
1.25 kg (2 lb 12 oz) potatoes
125 ml (4 fl oz/$\frac{1}{2}$ cup) reduced-fat milk
2 tbsp chopped parsley

PREP TIME: 40 MINUTES
COOKING TIME: 40 MINUTES
SERVES 4

Lightly spray a large non-stick frying pan with oil and place over medium heat. Add the onion, carrot and celery and stir constantly for 5 minutes, or until the vegetables begin to soften. Add 1 tablespoon water to prevent sticking. Remove the vegetables from the pan and set aside.

Spray the pan with a little more oil, add the lamb and cook over high heat until well browned. Add the flour and stir for 2–3 minutes. Return the vegetables to the pan and add the tomato paste, worcestershire sauce and stock. Stir and slowly bring to the boil. Reduce the heat, cover and simmer for 20 minutes, stirring occasionally.

Meanwhile, peel and chop the potatoes and cook until tender. Drain and mash until smooth. Add the milk, season with salt and pepper, then beat well.

Stir the parsley into the lamb and season well. Preheat a grill (broiler). Transfer the lamb into a 1.5 litre (52 fl oz/6 cup) baking dish. Spoon the potato over the top, spreading evenly with the back of a spoon. Use a fork to roughen up the potato and make the traditionally crunchy topping. Place under the grill and cook until the potato is golden, watching carefully because the potato browns quickly.

HINT:
• If preferred, divide the lamb mixture between individual ramekins before topping with the mashed potato.

nutrition per serve: Energy 1997 kJ (477 Cal); Fat 11.5 g; Saturated fat 4.5 g; Protein 37.9 g; Carbohydrate 50.9 g; Fibre 6.8 g; Cholesterol 90 mg

# BEEF STROGANOFF

STROGANOFF IS A DELICIOUS WINTER MEAL AND IS A GOOD SOURCE OF
PROTEIN AND THE MINERALS IRON AND ZINC.

500 g (1 lb 2 oz) lean rump steak, trimmed,
  thinly sliced
2 tbsp plain (all-purpose) flour
canola or olive oil spray
1 onion, sliced
250 g (9 oz) button mushrooms, halved
¼ tsp paprika
2 tbsp no-added-salt tomato paste
  (concentrated purée)

125 ml (4 fl oz/½ cup) reduced-salt
  beef stock
125 ml (4 fl oz/½ cup) extra-light
  sour cream
3 tbsp chopped parsley

PREP TIME: 20 MINUTES
COOKING TIME: 25 MINUTES
SERVES 4

Put the beef in a bowl with the flour and toss to coat, shaking off any excess. Spray a
non-stick frying pan with oil and place over high heat. Add the beef in batches and cook
for 3–4 minutes, or until just cooked through. Remove from the pan.

Lightly spray the pan and cook the onion, mushrooms and paprika over medium heat until
the onion has softened. Add the beef, tomato paste, stock and 125 ml (4 fl oz/½ cup)
water. Bring to the boil, then reduce the heat and simmer for 10 minutes.

Add the sour cream and half the parsley and stir to heat through. Season to taste with
freshly ground black pepper. Sprinkle with the remaining parsley and serve with rice
or pasta and steamed green vegetables.

nutrition per serve: Energy 1179 kJ (282 Cal); Fat 12.8 g; Saturated fat 5.1 g; Protein 31 g;
Carbohydrate 10.1 g; Fibre 2.8 g; Cholesterol 78 mg

# MINESTRONE

1 tbsp olive oil
1 onion, chopped
1 rindless bacon slice, finely chopped
3 carrots, halved lengthways and chopped
3 zucchini (courgettes), halved lengthways
  and chopped
2 celery stalks, sliced
2 potatoes, chopped
400 g (14 oz) tin no-added-salt diced
  tomatoes
300 g (10½ oz) tinned four-bean mix,
  drained and rinsed

30 g (1 oz/⅓ cup) small pasta shapes
125 g (4½ oz/1 cup) sliced green beans
grated parmesan cheese, to serve
chopped parsley, to serve

PREP TIME: 15 MINUTES
COOKING TIME: 1 HOUR 20 MINUTES
SERVES 6

Heat the oil in a large saucepan and sauté the onion and bacon until the onion is soft. Add the carrot, zucchini, celery, potato, tomato and bean mix and cook, stirring, for 1 minute.

Add 2.5 litres (87 fl oz/10 cups) water to the pan and season with freshly ground black pepper. Bring to the boil, then reduce the heat and simmer, covered, for 1 hour.

Stir in the pasta and beans and simmer for 12 minutes, or until tender. Sprinkle the minestrone with parmesan cheese and chopped parsley and serve with crusty bread.

THE COMBINATION OF MIXED
BEANS, VEGETABLES AND PASTA
MAKES THIS A FILLING AND
NUTRITIOUS MEAL FOR THE WHOLE
FAMILY. PREPARE THIS RECIPE
AHEAD OF TIME AND KEEP IT IN
THE REFRIGERATOR FOR A QUICK
WINTER DINNER OR LUNCH.

nutrition per serve: Energy 665 kJ (159 Cal)
Fat 4.3 g
Saturated fat 0.7 g
Protein 7.2 g
Carbohydrate 19.6 g
Fibre 6.3 g
Cholesterol 4 mg

# CHILLI CON CARNE

HIGHLY SALTED FOODS ARE EVERYWHERE TODAY, BUT THANKFULLY REDUCED- OR NO-ADDED-SALT ALTERNATIVES ARE NOW READILY AVAILABLE. TAKE THE TIME TO COMPARE LABELS TO SEE JUST HOW MUCH SALT THEY CAN SHED FROM YOUR FAMILY'S DIET.

2 tsp olive oil

1 large onion, chopped

1 garlic clove, crushed

½ tsp cayenne pepper, or to taste (optional)

2 tsp paprika

1 tsp dried oregano

2 tsp ground cumin

750 g (1 lb 10 oz) lean minced (ground) beef

375 ml (13 fl oz/1½ cups) reduced-salt beef stock

400 g (14 oz) tin no-added-salt diced tomatoes

125 g (4½ oz/½ cup) no-added-salt tomato paste (concentrated purée)

400 g (14 oz) tin kidney beans, rinsed and drained

low-fat plain yoghurt, to serve

PREP TIME: 15 MINUTES

COOKING TIME: 1 HOUR 10 MINUTES

SERVES 6

Heat the oil in a saucepan over low heat. Add the onion and cook for 4–5 minutes, or until soft. Stir in the garlic, cayenne pepper (if using), paprika, oregano and cumin. Increase the heat to medium, add the beef, stirring to break up the meat, and cook for 5–8 minutes, or until just browned.

Reduce the heat to low and add the stock, diced tomato and tomato paste and cook for 35–45 minutes, stirring frequently. Stir in the kidney beans and simmer for another 10 minutes. Serve the chilli con carne in small bowls over steamed rice or wrapped in pitta bread, with a green salad. Serve with a dollop of yoghurt.

nutrition per serve: Energy 1223 kJ (292 Cal); Fat 11.1 g; Saturated fat 3.6 g; Protein 32.4 g; Carbohydrate 13.3 g; Fibre 5.4 g; Cholesterol 76 mg

# RATATOUILLE

SERVE THIS HEALTHY VEGETABLE DISH WITH RICE OR CREAMY POLENTA FOR A TASTY GLUTEN-FREE MEAL. USED AS A SIDE DISH, IT IS ALSO A GREAT ACCOMPANIMENT TO LAMB.

6 tomatoes

3 tbsp olive oil

500 g (1 lb 2 oz) eggplant (aubergine), cut into 2 cm (¾ in) cubes

375 g (13 oz) zucchini (courgettes), cut into 2 cm (¾ in) cubes

1 green capsicum (pepper), cut into 2 cm (¾ in) cubes

1 red onion, cut into 2 cm (¾ in) wedges

3 garlic cloves, finely chopped

2 tsp chopped thyme

2 bay leaves

1 tbsp red wine vinegar

1 tsp caster (superfine) sugar

1 handful basil, shredded

PREP TIME: 30 MINUTES

COOKING TIME: 40 MINUTES

SERVES 4–6

To peel the tomatoes, score a cross in the base of each tomato, place in a heatproof bowl and cover with boiling water. Leave for 1 minute, or until the skins start to come away. Drain, plunge into a bowl of iced water, then peel away the skin. Roughly chop the flesh.

Heat 2 tablespoons of the oil in a large saucepan and cook the eggplant over medium heat for 4–5 minutes, or until soft but not browned. Remove from the pan.

Add the remaining oil to the pan, add the zucchini, capsicum and onion and cook for 3–4 minutes, or until the vegetables are softened. Add the garlic, thyme and bay leaves and cook, stirring, for 1 minute. Return the eggplant to the pan and add the tomato, vinegar and sugar. Simmer for 20 minutes, stirring occasionally. Stir in the basil and season to taste with salt and freshly ground black pepper.

HINTS:
- To decrease preparation time, substitute the fresh tomatoes with a 400 g (14 oz) tin no-added-salt diced tomatoes.
- For a quick and easy weeknight meal, any leftovers can be puréed in a food processor or blender and then used as a sauce for pasta or ravioli.

nutrition per serve (6): Energy 630 kJ (151 Cal); Fat 9.8 g; Saturated fat 1.3 g; Protein 4 g; Carbohydrate 8.7 g; Fibre 5 g; Cholesterol 0 mg

ONCE THEY TRY THEM, KIDS LOVE
THE NUTTY TASTE OF CHICKPEAS.
THEY ARE A GOOD SOURCE OF
VEGETABLE PROTEIN, SOLUBLE
FIBRE AND ANTIOXIDANTS.

nutrition per serve: Energy 289 kJ (69 Cal)

Fat 1.1 g

Saturated fat 0.1 g

Protein 4.3 g

Carbohydrate 8.6 g

Fibre 3.3 g

Cholesterol 0.4 mg

# CHICKPEA AND PARSLEY SALAD

**440 g (15½ oz) tin chickpeas**
**3 large tomatoes**
**2 tbsp chopped parsley**
**2 tsp chopped mint**
**2 tbsp lemon juice**
**2½ tbsp low-fat plain yoghurt**

PREP TIME: 10 MINUTES
COOKING TIME: NIL
SERVES 6

Drain the chickpeas, rinse under cold running water and drain again. Chop the tomatoes into 1 cm (½ in) pieces and put in a bowl with the drained chickpeas, parsley and mint.

In a small bowl, combine the lemon juice and yoghurt. Pour over the salad and mix until well combined. Serve as a vegetarian main with a green salad and crusty wholegrain bread or as a side dish for grilled fish or chicken.

# SWEET POTATO MASH

**300 g (10½ oz) orange sweet**
   **potato**
**2 tbsp extra-light sour cream**
**1–2 tbsp reduced-fat milk**

PREP TIME: 5 MINUTES
COOKING TIME: 5 MINUTES
SERVES 2 AS A SIDE DISH

Peel the sweet potato and cut into 3 cm (1¼ in) pieces. Boil, steam or microwave until soft. Mash the potato and stir in the sour cream and enough milk to make a soft mash.

nutrition per serve: Energy 525 kJ (125 Cal); Fat 2.8 g; Saturated fat 1.8 g; Protein 4 g; Carbohydrate 19.8 g; Fibre 2.2 g; Cholesterol 1.5 mg

# POTATO, PEA AND PARMESAN MASH

**250 g (9 oz) potatoes**
**80 g (2¾ oz/½ cup) frozen green peas**
**3 tbsp grated parmesan cheese**
**60 ml (2 fl oz/¼ cup) reduced-fat milk**

PREP TIME: 5 MINUTES
COOKING TIME: 10 MINUTES
SERVES 2 AS A SIDE DISH

Peel the potato and cut into 2 cm (¾ in) pieces. Place in a saucepan of cold water, bring to the boil, then add the peas and simmer for about 5 minutes or until the potatoes and peas are tender. Drain well. Mash roughly and then stir in the parmesan and enough milk to make a soft mash.

nutrition per serve: Energy 686 kJ (164 Cal); Fat 4 g; Saturated fat 2.4 g; Protein 10.1 g; Carbohydrate 19.4 g; Fibre 4.1 g; Cholesterol 12 mg

# PEAS, BACON AND LETTUCE

**115 g (4 oz/¾ cup) frozen green peas**
**1 tsp margarine**
**1 bacon slice, chopped**
**2 lettuce leaves, finely shredded**

PREP TIME: 5 MINUTES
COOKING TIME: 10 MINUTES
SERVES 2 AS A SIDE DISH

Cook the peas in a saucepan of boiling water for 5 minutes, or until tender, then drain. Melt the margarine in a small frying pan, add the bacon and stir over medium heat until softened and starting to brown. Add the lettuce and peas and stir until the lettuce has wilted.

nutrition per serve: Energy 588 kJ (141 Cal); Fat 9.4 g; Saturated fat 3.1 g; Protein 7.6 g; Carbohydrate 4.9 g; Fibre 3.6 g; Cholesterol 16 mg

# CAULIFLOWER MORNAY

**250 g (9 oz) cauliflower**
**2 tsp cornflour (cornstarch)**
**125 ml (4 fl oz/½ cup) reduced-fat milk**
**3 tbsp grated low-fat cheddar cheese**

PREP TIME: 5 MINUTES
COOKING TIME: 10 MINUTES
SERVES 2 AS A SIDE DISH

Cut the cauliflower into 3 cm (1¼ in) florets. Boil, steam or microwave until just tender, but take care not to overcook. Blend the cornflour and milk in a small saucepan, stir over medium heat until the mixture boils and thickens, then stir in 1 tablespoon of the cheese.

Place the cauliflower in a small heatproof dish, cover with the sauce and sprinkle with the remaining cheese. Place under a hot grill (broiler) until the cheese has melted and is golden brown.

nutrition per serve: Energy 459 kJ (110 Cal); Fat 2.6 g; Saturated fat 1.5 g; Protein 12 g; Carbohydrate 8.3 g; Fibre 2.3 g; Cholesterol 11 mg

# ROAST PUMPKIN WITH SOY SAUCE

**300 g (10½ oz) pumpkin (winter squash),**
  **cut into 4 wedges**
**2 tsp soy sauce**
**1 tsp olive oil**
**1 tsp sesame seeds**

PREP TIME: 5 MINUTES
COOKING TIME: 30 MINUTES
SERVES 2 AS A SIDE DISH

Preheat the oven to 200°C (400°F/Gas 6). Line a baking tray with baking paper.

Peel the pumpkin and make 3 mm (⅛ in) deep cuts in the top of each wedge, about 5 mm (¼ in) apart. Combine the soy sauce and olive oil. Place the wedges on the prepared tray and brush with half the soy and oil mixture.

Bake for 15 minutes, brush with the remaining soy and oil mixture and sprinkle with the sesame seeds. Bake for a further 15 minutes, or until tender.

ROASTING PUMPKIN BRINGS OUT ITS
NATURAL SWEETNESS, MAKING IT A
FIRM FAVOURITE WITH CHILDREN OF
ALL AGES.

nutrition per serve: Energy 330 kJ (79 Cal)
Fat 3.5 g
Saturated fat 0.8 g
Protein 3.1 g
Carbohydrate 7.8 g
Fibre 1.6 g
Cholesterol 0 mg

# PARTY FOOD

# CHEESE AND BACON TARTS

THESE DELICIOUS LITTLE TARTS ARE RICH WITH THE GOODNESS OF CHEESE
AND EGG. IF YOU LIKE YOU CAN SUBSTITUTE DRAINED AND FLAKED TINNED
SALMON FOR THE CHOPPED BACON.

**2 sheets ready-rolled shortcrust (pie)
  pastry
2 bacon slices, finely chopped
1 small onion, finely chopped
125 ml (4 fl oz/½ cup) light pouring
  cream
1 egg**

**½ tsp mild mustard
60 g (2¼ oz/½ cup) grated low-fat
  cheddar cheese**

PREP TIME: 30 MINUTES
COOKING TIME: 15 MINUTES
MAKES 18

Preheat the oven to 180°C (350°F/Gas 4). Lightly grease two 12-hole mini muffin tins.

Lay out the pastry on a lightly floured work surface. Cut out 18 rounds using a 7 cm (2¾ in)
fluted cutter. Ease the pastry rounds into the muffin holes. Sprinkle the chopped bacon
and onion over the pastry shells.

Combine the cream, egg and mustard in a small bowl and whisk until smooth. Spoon
1 teaspoon of the mixture into each pastry case and sprinkle with the grated cheese.
Bake the tarts for 15 minutes, or until golden and crisp. Serve warm.

HINT:
• Use reduced-fat shortcrust pastry to lower the fat content of the tarts further. If you
  can't find a lower fat pastry, choose a brand that uses healthier fats such as canola or
  sunflower oil.

nutrition per tart: Energy 399 kJ (95 Cal); Fat 6 g; Saturated fat 3.3 g; Protein 3.5 g;
Carbohydrate 6.8 g; Fibre 0.3 g; Cholesterol 22 mg

# SAUSAGE ROLLS

PREPARED AHEAD OF TIME AND THEN FROZEN, HOME-MADE SAUSAGE ROLLS
ARE AS CONVENIENT AS COMMERCIAL ONES, WHILE HAVING THE ADDED
BENEFIT OF BEING LOWER IN SALT AND FAT.

**1 tsp oil**

**1 onion, finely chopped**

**500 g (1 lb 2 oz) minced (ground) sausage
meat**

**80 g (2¾ oz/1 cup) fresh breadcrumbs**

**2 tbsp tomato sauce (ketchup)**

**1 egg, lightly beaten**

**2 sheets frozen ready-rolled puff pastry,
thawed**

**beaten egg or milk, for glazing**

**tomato sauce or home-made tomato
sauce (page 102), to serve**

PREP TIME: 35 MINUTES

COOKING TIME: 30 MINUTES

MAKES 48

Preheat the oven to 210°C (415°F/Gas 6–7). Lightly grease a baking tray with oil.

Heat the oil in a frying pan, add the onion and cook over low heat for 2–3 minutes, or until soft and transparent. Put the onion, meat, breadcrumbs, tomato sauce and egg into a bowl and mix together.

Lay the pastry sheets on a lightly floured work surface and cut each into three horizontal strips. Divide the meat mixture into six equal portions and place across the long edge of the pastry. Roll the pastry up to form long sausage shapes. Brush lightly with a little beaten egg or milk. Cut the rolls into 4 cm (1½ in) lengths and place on the prepared tray.

Bake for 10 minutes, then reduce the heat to 180°C (350°F/Gas 4) and bake for a further 15 minutes, or until golden. Serve with tomato sauce, for dipping.

HINTS:
• These sausage rolls can be frozen for up to 2 weeks before serving. Thaw and reheat them in a 180°C (350°F/Gas 4) oven for 15–20 minutes, or until hot.
• If desired, use reduced-fat puff pastry to lower the fat content of the rolls further.

nutrition per sausage roll: Energy 223 kJ (53 Cal); Fat 2.9 g; Saturated fat 1.3 g; Protein 2.8 g;
Carbohydrate 4 g; Fibre 0.2 g; Cholesterol 13 mg

THESE CHICKEN NUGGETS USE
PREMIUM INGREDIENTS THAT ARE
TASTY AS WELL AS NUTRITIOUS.
THEY MAKE GREAT PARTY FOOD, OR
YOU CAN SERVE THEM AS A MAIN
MEAL WITH VEGETABLES OR A
GREEN SALAD.

nutrition per nugget: Energy 106 kJ (25 Cal)
Fat 1.2 g
Saturated fat 0.3 g
Protein 2.6 g
Carbohydrate 1.1 g
Fibre 0.04 g
Cholesterol 17 mg

# BAKED CHICKEN NUGGETS

**375 g (13 oz) boneless, skinless chicken
thighs, roughly chopped**
**1 egg**
**1 tbsp snipped chives**
**¼ tsp sesame oil**
**2 tsp plum sauce**

**1 tsp reduced-salt soy sauce**
**30 g (1 oz/1 cup) cornflakes**

PREP TIME: 20 MINUTES
COOKING TIME: 15 MINUTES
MAKES ABOUT 30 NUGGETS

Preheat the oven to 180°C (350°F/Gas 4). Line a baking tray with foil and lightly grease with oil.

Put the chicken, egg, chives, sesame oil, plum sauce and soy sauce in a food processor and process for 30 seconds, or until the mixture is smooth.

Shape heaped teaspoons of the mixture into balls. Roll the balls in the cornflakes, then place on the prepared tray. Bake for 15 minutes, or until the chicken nuggets are golden and crisp. Serve with plum or tomato sauce for dipping.

# VEGIE PUFFS

THESE TASTY PASTRIES LOOK JUST LIKE SAUSAGE ROLLS EXCEPT THEY ARE PACKED WITH THE GOODNESS OF VEGETABLES AND CHEESE. THEY MAKE GREAT PARTY FOOD OR SERVE THEM WITH PUMPKIN OR VEGETABLE SOUP FOR DINNER OR A WEEKEND LUNCH.

1 small potato, peeled and diced

1 small carrot, peeled and diced

1 small zucchini (courgette), diced

1 small celery stalk, diced

50 g (1¾ oz/⅓ cup) diced pumpkin (winter squash)

40 g (1½ oz/½ cup) chopped broccoli

185 g (6½ oz/1½ cups) grated low-fat cheddar cheese

2 sheets frozen ready-rolled puff pastry, thawed and halved

1 tbsp reduced-fat milk, for brushing

PREP TIME: 15 MINUTES

COOKING TIME: 15 MINUTES

MAKES 24 PUFFS

Put the vegetables in a small saucepan with enough water to cover. Bring to the boil, then reduce the heat and simmer for 3 minutes, or until tender. Drain well and transfer to a bowl to cool. Add the cheese and mix well.

Preheat the oven to 220°C (425°F/Gas 7). Lightly grease two baking trays.

Lay the four pieces of pastry on a work surface, divide the mixture in quarters and spread it along the long side of each piece. Roll up the pastry to form a sausage shape, brush the edge with a little milk and press to seal.

Cut each roll into six even-sized pieces. Make a small slit in the centre of each and place on the prepared trays. Brush with milk and bake for 10 minutes, or until crisp and golden.

HINT:
• Look for a puff pastry made with healthy fats such as canola or sunflower oil.

nutrition per vegie puff: Energy 304 kJ (73 Cal); Fat 3.8 g; Saturated fat 2.1 g; Protein 3.7 g; Carbohydrate 5.8 g; Fibre 0.5 g; Cholesterol 6 mg

# MEATBALLS

BITE-SIZED, TASTY MEATBALLS ARE QUICK AND EASY TO EAT—IMPORTANT WHEN THE DISTRACTION OF PARTY PLAY IS SO GREAT. SERVE THEM WITH THE TOMATO MAYONNAISE FOR DIPPING OR OFFER A VARIETY OF SAUCES SUCH AS PLUM SAUCE OR HOME-MADE TOMATO SAUCE (PAGE 102).

**TOMATO MAYONNAISE**
**90 ml (3 fl oz) tomato sauce (ketchup)**
**90 ml (3 fl oz) mayonnaise**
**½ tsp finely chopped dill or parsley**
**½ garlic clove, crushed**

**375 g (13 oz) lean minced (ground) beef**
**1 small onion, finely chopped**
**40 g (1½ oz/½ cup) fresh breadcrumbs**

**1 tbsp no-added-salt tomato paste**
  **(concentrated purée)**
**1 tsp worcestershire sauce**
**1 egg, lightly beaten**
**2 tbsp oil**

PREP TIME: 20 MINUTES
COOKING TIME: 10 MINUTES
MAKES 25

To make the tomato mayonnaise, combine the tomato sauce, mayonnaise, dill or parsley and garlic in a bowl until well combined. Set aside.

Put the beef, onion, breadcrumbs, tomato paste, worcestershire sauce and egg in a large bowl. Using your hands, mix until well combined. Shape level tablespoons of the mixture into balls.

Heat the oil in a large frying pan. Add the meatballs and cook over medium heat, shaking the pan often, for 10 minutes, or until the meatballs are cooked and evenly browned. Drain on paper towels. Serve hot or cold with the tomato mayonnaise.

nutrition per meatball: Energy 254 kJ (61 Cal); Fat 3.7 g; Saturated fat 0.8 g; Protein 3.7 g; Carbohydrate 3 g; Fibre 0.2 g; Cholesterol 16 mg

# GLAZED DRUMETTES

**16 chicken drumettes (see Hint)**
**80 ml (2½ fl oz/⅓ cup) golden syrup or**
   **honey**
**60 ml (2 fl oz/¼ cup) pear or apple juice**
**1 tbsp canola oil**

PREP TIME: 20 MINUTES + OVERNIGHT
   MARINATING
COOKING TIME: 25 MINUTES
MAKES 16

Put the chicken drumettes in a shallow non-metallic dish. Combine the remaining ingredients and pour over the drumettes, making sure they are well coated. Marinate overnight, turning occasionally.

Preheat the oven to 180°C (350°F/Gas 4). Transfer the drumettes and marinade to a baking tin. Bake for 20–25 minutes, turning frequently during cooking and brushing with the cooking juices. If the juices start to brown too much, add a small amount of water or stock until syrupy. Serve hot or cold at parties or picnics, or as a main meal with a green salad and rice.

HINT:
• Chicken drumettes are available from most supermarkets and chicken shops. They are simply the small fleshy part of the chicken wing, with the tip removed.

SMALL CHICKEN PIECES ARE
EASY-TO-EAT FOOD FOR
CHILDREN AND ARE A GREAT
PARTY FAVOURITE. THIS RECIPE
IS FREE OF EGG, DAIRY,
GLUTEN, NUT AND SOY.

nutrition per drumette: Energy 574 kJ (137 Cal)

Fat 9.3 g

Saturated fat 2.4 g

Protein 8.3 g

Carbohydrate 5.7 g

Fibre 0 g

Cholesterol 43 mg

# PORK AND CHIVE DUMPLINGS

THESE CAN BE MADE AHEAD OF TIME AND FROZEN, THEN ON THE DAY OF THE
PARTY, ALL YOU NEED TO DO IS COOK THEM. CHILDREN WILL LOVE TO HELP
PREPARE THESE TASTY LITTLE DUMPLINGS.

**1 tsp vegetable oil**
**2 garlic cloves, crushed**
**2 tsp finely grated ginger**
**30 g (1 oz/1 bunch) chives, snipped**
**½ carrot, finely diced**
**200 g (7 oz) minced (ground) pork**
**2 tbsp oyster sauce**
**2 tsp reduced-salt soy sauce**

**½ tsp sesame oil**
**1 tsp cornflour (cornstarch)**
**24 round gow gee wrappers**

PREP TIME: 45 MINUTES
COOKING TIME: 15 MINUTES
MAKES 24

Heat a wok over high heat, add the oil and swirl to coat the base and side of the wok. Add the garlic, ginger, chives and carrot, then stir-fry for 2 minutes, or until fragrant. Remove the wok from the heat and allow to cool.

Meanwhile, put the pork, oyster sauce, soy sauce, sesame oil and cornflour in a bowl and mix well. Add the cooled vegetable mixture, mixing it into the pork until well combined.

Put 2 teaspoons of the mixture in the centre of a gow gee wrapper. Moisten the edge with water, then fold in half to form a semi-circle. Pinch along the edge at 5 mm (¼ in) intervals to form a ruffled edge. Repeat with the remaining filling and wrappers.

Line a double bamboo steamer (or work in two batches with a single steamer) with baking paper. Put half the dumplings in a single layer in each steamer basket. Cover and steam over a wok of simmering water for 12 minutes, or until cooked through. Serve with your child's favourite dipping sauce.

nutrition per dumpling: Energy 179 kJ (43 Cal); Fat 1.1 g; Saturated fat 0.2 g; Protein 2.6 g; Carbohydrate 5.2 g; Fibre 0.3 g; Cholesterol 3 mg

# MONEY BAGS

THESE LITTLE PARCELS ARE A FUN EASY-TO-EAT FOOD WITH A GREAT CRUNCH FACTOR.

1 tbsp peanut oil
4 spring onions (scallions), finely chopped
2 garlic cloves, crushed
1 tbsp grated fresh ginger
150 g (5½ oz) minced (ground) chicken
150 g (5½ oz) minced (ground) pork
2 tsp reduced-salt soy sauce
2 tsp soft brown sugar
2 tsp lime juice (optional)
2 tsp fish sauce (optional)

3 tbsp finely chopped coriander (cilantro) leaves
30 won ton wrappers
oil, for deep-frying
garlic chives, for tying (optional)

PREP TIME: 40 MINUTES
COOKING TIME: 15 MINUTES
MAKES 30

Heat a wok over medium heat, add the oil and swirl to coat the base and side. Add the spring onion, garlic and ginger and cook for 1–2 minutes. Add the chicken and pork and cook for 4 minutes, breaking up the lumps with the back of a spoon.

Stir in the soy sauce, sugar, lime juice and fish sauce, if using, and coriander. Cook, stirring, for 1–2 minutes, or until mixed and dry. Set aside to cool.

Place 2 teaspoons of the filling in the centre of each won ton wrapper, then lightly brush the edges with water. Lift the sides up tightly and pinch around the filling to form a bag.

Fill a clean wok one-third full of oil and heat to 190°C (375°F), or until a cube of bread dropped into the oil browns in 10 seconds. Cook the money bags in the hot oil in batches for 30–60 seconds, or until golden and crisp. Drain on crumpled paper towels, then tie with the chives if desired.

nutrition per money bag: Energy 238 kJ (57 Cal); Fat 2.7 g; Saturated fat 0.5 g; Protein 2.9 g; Carbohydrate 4.9 g; Fibre 0.3 g; Cholesterol 7 mg

WE ALL NEED TO LIMIT THE AMOUNT OF SATURATED FAT IN OUR DIETS— EVEN CHILDREN. MAKING THESE CAKES WITH MARGARINE INSTEAD OF BUTTER MAKES A BIG DIFFERENCE TO THE SATURATED FAT CONTENT WITHOUT AFFECTING THE FLAVOUR.

nutrition per cupcake: Energy 989 kJ (236 Cal)
Fat 11.7 g
Saturated fat 3.8 g
Protein 3.8 g
Carbohydrate 29.6 g
Fibre 0.6 g
Cholesterol 41 mg

**156**

# BUTTERFLY CUPCAKES

125 g (4½ oz) margarine, softened
170 g (6 oz/¾ cup) caster (superfine) sugar
185 g (6½ oz/1½ cups) self-raising flour
125 ml (4 fl oz/½ cup) reduced-fat milk
2 eggs
80 ml (2½ fl oz/⅓ cup) pouring
   (whipping) cream
80 g (2¾ oz/⅓ cup) low-fat ricotta cheese

2 tsp icing (confectioners') sugar, plus
   extra, to dust
2 tbsp strawberry jam

PREP TIME: 15 MINUTES

COOKING TIME: 20 MINUTES

MAKES 12

Preheat the oven to 180°C (350°F/Gas 4). Line the holes of two 12-hole standard muffin tins with paper cases.

Beat the margarine, sugar, flour, milk and eggs with electric beaters on low speed until combined. Increase the speed and beat until smooth and pale. Divide the mixture evenly among the cases and bake for 15–20 minutes, or until cooked and golden. Transfer to a wire rack to cool.

Put the cream in a small bowl and beat until slightly thickened, then add the ricotta and icing sugar and beat until the mixture is smooth and thickened.

Cut shallow rounds from the centre of each cupcake using the point of a sharp knife, then cut the rounds in half. Spoon 2 teaspoons of the ricotta cream into each cavity, top with a little strawberry jam and position the two halves of the cake tops in the jam to resemble butterfly wings. Dust with the extra icing sugar.

# STRAWBERRY AND JAM-FILLED CAKES

THESE LITTLE CAKES CLEVERLY CONCEAL A STRAWBERRY SURPRISE. YOU CAN USE PURÉED FRUIT OR JAM OF ANY TYPE.

280 g (10 oz/2¼ cups) self-raising flour
170 g (6 oz/¾ cup) caster (superfine) sugar
250 ml (9 fl oz/1 cup) reduced-fat milk
2 eggs, lightly beaten
½ tsp natural vanilla extract
75 g (2½ oz) margarine, melted
80 g (2¾ oz/¼ cup) strawberry jam

12 small strawberries, hulled
icing (confectioners') sugar, for dusting

PREP TIME: 10 MINUTES
COOKING TIME: 20 MINUTES
MAKES 12

Preheat the oven to 200°C (400°F/Gas 6). Grease a 12-hole standard muffin tin.

Sift the flour into a bowl, add the sugar and stir to combine. Make a well in the centre. Put the milk, eggs, vanilla and margarine in a bowl, whisking to combine. Pour into the well and, using a metal spoon, gradually fold the milk mixture into the flour mixture until just combined.

Divide three-quarters of the cake mixture among the muffin holes. Top each one with 1 teaspoon of the jam and cover with the remaining cake batter. Gently press a strawberry into the centre.

Bake for 20 minutes, or until light golden. Cool in the tin for 5 minutes, then turn out onto a wire rack to cool completely. Dust with icing sugar to serve. The cakes are best served on the day they are made.

nutrition per cake: Energy 932 kJ (223 Cal); Fat 5.8 g; Saturated fat 1.3 g; Protein 4.3 g; Carbohydrate 38.5 g; Fibre 1.1 g; Cholesterol 33 mg

# YOGHURT BANANA CAKES WITH HONEY ICING

THIS RECIPE WILL MAKE TWO CAKES, WHICH CAN BE DECORATED AS BIRTHDAY CAKES, OR YOU CAN COOK THE MIXTURE INTO INDIVIDUAL CUPCAKES.

180 g (6 oz) margarine, softened
90 g (3¼ oz/¼ cup) honey
230 g (8 oz/1 cup) caster (superfine) sugar
1½ tsp natural vanilla extract
3 eggs
360 g (12¾ oz/1½ cups) mashed ripe
　banana (about 4 bananas)
185 g (6½ oz/¾ cup) low-fat plain yoghurt
½ tsp bicarbonate of soda (baking soda)
375 g (13 oz/3 cups) self-raising flour, sifted

**HONEY ICING**
125 g (4½ oz/1 cup) icing (confectioners')
　sugar
1 tbsp honey
1–2 tbsp warm milk or water

PREP TIME: 15 MINUTES
COOKING TIME: 1 HOUR
MAKES 56 CUPCAKES, OR 2 LARGE CAKES

Preheat the oven to 180°C (350°F/Gas 4). Lightly grease a flat-bottomed patty cake tin and line with paper cases. If making two large cakes, lightly grease two 15 cm (6 inch) round cake tins and line the bases with baking paper.

Cream the margarine, honey, sugar and vanilla in a bowl using electric beaters until pale and fluffy. Add the eggs one at a time, beating well after each addition, then beat in the banana.

Combine the yoghurt and bicarbonate of soda in a small bowl. Fold the flour alternately with the yoghurt into the banana mixture. Divide the mixture evenly between the paper cases or the cake tins. Bake for 18–20 minutes for the cupcakes, or 50–60 minutes for the large cakes, or until a skewer inserted into the centre comes out clean. Cool in the tins for 5 minutes, then turn out onto a wire rack.

To make the honey icing, put the icing sugar in a small bowl. Melt the honey in the microwave or a saucepan over low heat until runny, then add to the icing sugar. Gradually add the milk or water, a little at a time, stirring until the mixture is smooth and coats the back of the spoon. When the cakes are cold, drizzle them with the honey icing.

HINT:
• These cakes will keep, stored in an airtight container, for up to 4 days. Un-iced cakes can be frozen for up to 3 months.

nutrition per cupcake (56): Energy 371 kJ (88 Cal); Fat 2.6 g; Saturated fat 0.5 g; Protein 1.3 g; Carbohydrate 15.1 g; Fibre 0.4 g; Cholesterol 10 mg

**159**

# MERINGUE KISSES

**pure maize cornflour (cornstarch),
for dusting**
**60 ml (2 fl oz/¼ cup) egg white (about
2 egg whites)**
**145 g (5 oz/⅔ cup) superfine (caster) sugar**
**1 tsp pure icing (confectioners') sugar**

**melted chocolate, to serve (optional)**
**whipped cream, to serve (optional)**

PREP TIME: 20 MINUTES

COOKING TIME: 40 MINUTES

MAKES ABOUT 20 SINGLE MERINGUES

Preheat the oven to 120°C (235°F/Gas 1). Lightly grease two baking trays, then dust them lightly with cornflour.

Combine the egg whites, caster sugar and a pinch of salt in the small bowl of an electric mixer. Beat on high speed for 10–12 minutes. Gently fold in the icing sugar.

Spoon the meringue into a piping bag fitted with a fluted tube. Pipe stars or rosettes onto the prepared trays. Bake for about 40 minutes, or until the meringues feel firm and dry. Allow to cool in the oven with the door ajar.

If desired, dip half of the meringues in melted chocolate. When the chocolate has hardened, sandwich together with whipped cream.

HINT:
• This is a basic meringue mixture. It makes small crisp meringues that store well in an airtight container. For best results measure your egg whites. The amount must be accurate to fully absorb the quantity of sugar.
• If making these meringues for children on a gluten-free diet, make sure you use pure icing sugar. Soft icing sugar or icing sugar mixtures can contain cornflour with wheat starch in it. Similarly, if dipping in chocolate, ensure the chocolate is gluten-free.

IT'S NOT UNUSUAL TO HAVE
CHILDREN WITH SPECIAL FOOD
NEEDS AT YOUR PARTIES THESE
DAYS. BY USING GLUTEN-FREE
ICING SUGAR AND CORNFLOUR,
THESE MERINGUE KISSES ARE
GREAT FOR CHILDREN WHO ARE
WHEAT OR GLUTEN INTOLERANT.

nutrition per meringue (20): Energy 127 kJ (30 Cal)
Fat 0 g
Saturated fat 0 g
Protein 0.4 g
Carbohydrate 7.5 g
Fibre 0 g
Cholesterol 0 mg

**161**

# GINGERBREAD PEOPLE

MAKE UP THE DOUGH AND PASS IT ON TO YOUR 'HELPERS' TO ROLL AND CUT OUT. ONCE THE BISCUITS ARE BAKED AND COOL, THE CHILDREN CAN HAVE LOTS OF FUN DECORATING THEM.

125 g (4½ oz) margarine
90 g (3¼ oz/½ cup) soft brown sugar
115 g (4 oz/⅓ cup) golden syrup or dark
   corn syrup
1 egg
250 g (9 oz/2 cups) plain (all-purpose)
   flour
40 g (1½ oz/⅓ cup) self-raising flour
2–3 tsp ground ginger, to taste
1 tsp bicarbonate of soda
   (baking soda)

ICING (FROSTING)
1 egg white
½ tsp lemon juice
125 g (4½ oz/1 cup) icing (confectioners')
   sugar
food colourings

PREP TIME: 30 MINUTES + 15 MINUTES
   REFRIGERATION
COOKING TIME: 15 MINUTES
MAKES 15–20, DEPENDING ON SIZE OF CUTTERS

Line two or three baking trays with baking paper. Using electric beaters, beat the margarine, sugar and golden syrup in a large bowl until light and creamy. Add the egg and beat well. Sift in the flours, ginger and bicarbonate of soda. Use a knife to mix until just combined. Use a well-floured hand to gather the dough into a ball. Knead gently on a well-floured surface until smooth. Don't over-handle the dough or it will become tough.

Lay a sheet of baking paper over a large chopping board. Roll out the dough on the lined board to a 5 mm (¼ in) thickness. Preheat the oven to 180°C (350°F/Gas 4).

Refrigerate the dough on the board for 15 minutes, or until it is firm enough to cut. Cut the dough into shapes using assorted gingerbread people cutters. Press any remaining dough together, re-roll and cut out into shapes.

Bake the gingerbread for 10–12 minutes, or until lightly browned. Cool the biscuits on the trays, then decorate with the icing.

To make the icing, beat the egg white in a small bowl with electric beaters until soft peaks form. Gradually add the lemon juice and sifted icing sugar and beat until thick and creamy. Divide the icing into several bowls and tint with food colourings. Spoon into small paper icing bags and use to decorate the biscuits.

nutrition per biscuit (20): Energy 633 kJ (151 Cal); Fat 4.8 g; Saturated fat 0.9 g; Protein 2.1 g; Carbohydrate 25.3 g; Fibre 0.6 g; Cholesterol 9 mg

# THUMBPRINT BISCUITS

PARTY FOOD IS ALL ABOUT 'SOMETIMES' FOODS. BUT, IF YOU HAVE THE TIME TO MAKE THESE FOODS YOURSELF YOU ARE AT LEAST ABLE TO INFLUENCE THE AMOUNT OF FAT, SALT AND SUGAR YOUR CHILDREN END UP EATING.

**250 g (9 oz) margarine, softened**
**140 g (5 oz) icing (confectioners') sugar**
**1 egg yolk, lightly beaten**
**90 g (3¼ oz) light cream cheese, softened**
**and cut into chunks**
**1½ tsp natural vanilla extract**
**1 tsp finely grated lemon zest**
**350 g (12 oz/2¾ cups) plain (all-purpose)**
**flour, sifted**
**¼ tsp baking powder**

**½ tsp bicarbonate of soda (baking soda)**
**2 tbsp each apricot, blueberry and**
**raspberry jam**

PREP TIME: 30 MINUTES + 10 MINUTES
STANDING
COOKING TIME: 15 MINUTES
MAKES ABOUT 45

Preheat the oven to 180°C (350°F/Gas 4). Lightly grease three baking trays.

Cream the margarine, icing sugar and egg yolk in a bowl using electric beaters until pale and fluffy, then beat in the cream cheese, vanilla and lemon zest until smooth. Combine the flour, baking powder, bicarbonate of soda and ¼ teaspoon salt in a large bowl and, using a wooden spoon, gradually stir into the creamed mixture until a soft dough forms. Set aside for 5–10 minutes, or until the dough firms up.

Break off small (15 g/½ oz) pieces of dough, shape into balls and flatten slightly to make 4 cm (1½ in) rounds. Transfer to the prepared trays and make a small indent in the centre of each with your thumb. Spoon about ¼ teaspoon of apricot jam into one-third of the biscuits, ¼ teaspoon blueberry jam into one-third, and ¼ teaspoon of raspberry jam into the remaining one-third of the biscuits. Bake for 10–12 minutes, or until light golden. Cool for a few minutes on the trays, then transfer to a wire rack.

HINT:
• These biscuits are best eaten the same day but will keep, stored in an airtight container, for up to 2 days.

nutrition per biscuit: Energy 371 kJ (89 Cal); Fat 4.4 g; Saturated fat 1 g; Protein 1.1 g; Carbohydrate 11.2 g; Fibre 0.3 g; Cholesterol 5 mg

THESE BISCUITS CAN BE MADE UP
TO A WEEK AHEAD OF TIME AND
STORED IN AN AIRTIGHT CONTAINER,
AND THEN DECORATED ON THE DAY
OF THE PARTY.

nutrition per biscuit: Energy 1072 kJ (256 Cal)

Fat 9.5 g

Saturated fat 1.7 g

Protein 2.9 g

Carbohydrate 40.6 g

Fibre 0.8 g

Cholesterol 19 mg

# SPRINKLE BISCUITS

**125 g (4½ oz) margarine, softened**
**115 g (4 oz/½ cup) caster (superfine) sugar**
**1 egg**
**210 g (7½ oz/1¾ cups) plain (all-purpose)**
**flour**
**125 g (4½ oz/1 cup) icing (confectioners')**
**sugar**

**food colouring**
**assorted sprinkles**

PREP TIME: 20 MINUTES + 30 MINUTES
REFRIGERATION
COOKING TIME: 15 MINUTES
MAKES 10

To make the biscuits, beat the margarine, sugar and egg using electric beaters until light and creamy. Add the flour and, using your hands, press the mixture together to form a soft dough. Turn onto a lightly floured work surface and knead for 2 minutes, or until smooth. Refrigerate, covered with plastic wrap, for 30 minutes.

Preheat the oven to 180°C (350°F/Gas 4). Lightly grease a baking tray.

Roll the dough between two sheets of baking paper to a 5 mm (¼ in) thickness. Cut into shapes using a cutter of your choice. Place on the prepared tray and bake for 15 minutes, or until golden. Leave to cool a little on the tray before transferring to a wire rack.

Place the sifted icing sugar in a bowl. Add 3 tablespoons hot water and a few drops of food colouring and stir until well combined. Dip the front of each biscuit into the icing, holding the biscuits over the bowl to allow any excess icing to drip off. While the icing is still soft, decorate with the sprinkles as desired.

# CHOC-CHIP CRACKLES

THESE CRUNCHY TREATS, FILLED WITH SULTANAS AND CHOCOLATE CHIPS, WILL BE FULL OF SURPRISES FOR YOUNG PARTY-GOERS. BECAUSE THERE IS NO BAKING INVOLVED THEY ARE ALSO GREAT FOR THE KIDS TO HELP PREPARE.

90 g (3¼ oz/3 cups) puffed rice cereal
30 g (1 oz/¼ cup) unsweetened cocoa
  powder
150 g (5½ oz/1¼ cups) icing
  (confectioners') sugar
60 g (2¼ oz/½ cup) sultanas (golden
  raisins)
60 g (2¼ oz/⅔ cup) desiccated coconut

200 g (7 oz) Copha (white vegetable
  shortening), melted
60 g (2¼ oz/⅓ cup) dark choc chips

PREP TIME: 20 MINUTES
COOKING TIME: 5 MINUTES
MAKES 24

Line two 12-hole mini muffin tins with foil cases. Combine the puffed rice cereal, cocoa and icing sugar in a large bowl. Mix thoroughly, then stir in the sultanas and coconut. Stir in the melted shortening.

Spoon the mixture into the prepared muffin tins. Sprinkle with the choc chips and refrigerate until set.

nutrition per crackle: Energy 638 kJ (152 Cal); Fat 10.9 g; Saturated fat 9.7 g; Protein 0.8 g; Carbohydrate 13.2 g; Fibre 0.6 g; Cholesterol 0.1 mg

# FRUIT JELLIES

IF YOU DON'T HAVE JELLY MOULDS, MAKE THE JELLIES IN CLEAR GLASSES, AND SERVE IN THE GLASSES WITH A SPOON. SERVE WITH LOW-FAT FRUIT YOGHURT IF DESIRED.

**500 ml (17 fl oz/2 cups) cranberry and raspberry juice**
**4 teaspoons gelatine**
**330 g (11½ oz) mixed berries, fresh or frozen**

PREP TIME: 20 MINUTES + REFRIGERATION
COOKING TIME: NIL
SERVES 4

Put 60 ml (2 fl oz/¼ cup) of the juice in a small bowl, sprinkle over the gelatine in an even layer and leave to go spongy. Bring a small saucepan of water to the boil, remove from the heat and place the bowl in the pan. The water should come halfway up the side of the bowl. Stir the gelatine until clear and dissolved. Cool slightly and mix with the rest of the juice.

Rinse four 185 ml (6 fl oz/¾ cup) moulds with water (wet moulds make it easier when unmoulding) and pour 2 cm (¾ in) of the juice into each. Refrigerate until set.

Meanwhile, if the berries are frozen, thaw them and add any liquid to the remaining juice. When the bottom layer of jelly has set, divide the fruit among the moulds (reserving a few berries to garnish) and divide the rest of the juice among the moulds, pouring it over the fruit. Refrigerate until set.

To turn out the jellies, hold each mould in a hot, damp tea towel (dish towel) and turn out onto a plate. Ease away the edge of the jelly with your finger to break the seal. (If you turn the jellies onto a damp plate you will be able to move them around, otherwise they will stick.) Garnish with the reserved berries.

HINT:
• Cranberry and raspberry juice is available from most large supermarkets. Use a similar juice such as cranberry and blackcurrant if unavailable.

nutrition per serve: Energy 369 kJ (88 Cal); Fat 0.2 g; Saturated fat 0.04 g; Protein 4.3 g; Carbohydrate 16.3 g; Fibre 2.5 g; Cholesterol 0 mg

# PARTY CUPCAKE

300 g (10½ oz) margarine, softened
575 g (1 lb 4 oz/2½ cups) caster
   (superfine) sugar
6 eggs
435 g (15¼ oz/3½ cups) self-raising flour
60 g (2¼ oz/½ cup) custard powder
250 ml (9 fl oz/1 cup) reduced-fat milk
1 tbsp finely grated orange zest
125 ml (4 fl oz/½ cup) orange juice
500 g (1 lb 2 oz) packet ready-made
   soft icing
licorice straps and sweets, for decoration

**ICING (FROSTING)**
80 g (2¾ oz) margarine, softened
375 g (13 oz/3 cups) icing (confectioners')
   sugar mixture
2–3 tbsp orange juice
food colouring of your choice

PREP TIME: 30 MINUTES + 1½ HOURS FOR
   DECORATION
COOKING TIME: 1 HOUR 10 MINUTES
SERVES ABOUT 20

Preheat the oven to 180°C (350°F/Gas 4). Lightly grease two deep 20 cm (8 in) round cake tins and line the bases and sides with baking paper.

Combine the margarine, sugar, eggs, flour, custard powder, milk, orange zest and juice in the large bowl of an electric mixer. Mix on low speed until the ingredients are just combined, then increase the speed to medium and beat for about 3 minutes, or until lightened in colour. Spread the cake mixture into the prepared tins and bake for about 1 hour 10 minutes, or until the cakes are cooked when tested with a skewer (cover with foil after 1 hour if they start browning too much). Cool in the tins for 5 minutes, then turn out onto wire racks to cool, leaving the cakes rounded side up.

To make the icing, beat the margarine, icing sugar and orange juice in a small bowl with an electric mixer until as light as possible. Tint the icing, then cover and set aside.

Cut the rounded top off one of the cakes, spread the cake with a little icing, then top with the remaining cake, rounded side up. Using a serrated knife, trim a little off the edge of the top cake to define a rounded top. Then cut the sides of the cake down from the top rounded edge of the cake at an angle to represent the sides of a cupcake.

Dust the work surface with icing sugar and knead the soft icing to soften. Tint the icing the colour of your choice, kneading the colour through the icing. Roll out into a rectangle with a rolling pin to 4 mm (¼ in) thick. You will need to cut two strips of icing about 30 cm (12 in) long and 2 cm (¾ in) higher than the side of the cake. Make vertical impressions in the icing with the back of a knife to represent a paper patty case, and indent along the top edge a little to form the rippled look of the rim. Spread some of the icing over the side of the cake and gently press the strips of soft icing onto the icing to look like a paper patty case, trimming at the joins. Spread the remaining icing over the top. Form the number of the child's birthday using licorice straps and decorate with the sweets, as desired.

THE FINALE TO ANY CHILD'S
PARTY IS ALWAYS THE CAKE, AND
THIS BRIGHTLY DECORATED
GIANT 'CUPCAKE' IS SURE TO BE
A HIT. MAKE THE CAKE A DAY
AHEAD, THEN DECORATE IT ON
THE DAY OF THE PARTY.

nutrition per serve (20): Energy 1405 kJ (336 Cal)

Fat 10.7 g

Saturated fat 2.8 g

Protein 3.1 g

Carbohydrate 58.1 g

Fibre 0.6 g

Cholesterol 37 mg

# DESSERTS

# YOGHURT JELLY

THIS EASY-TO-MAKE JELLY IS LOW IN FAT AND KILOJOULES AND PROVIDES SOME VITAMIN C PLUS THE IMPORTANT MINERALS, CALCIUM AND PHOSPHORUS. USE A GREEK-STYLE YOGHURT FOR AN EXTRA CREAMY VERSION.

1½ tbsp gelatine powder
375 ml (13 fl oz/1½ cups) unsweetened
    fruit juice
250 g (9 oz/1 cup) low-fat plain yoghurt

PREP TIME: 10 MINUTES
COOKING TIME: 5 MINUTES
SERVES 6

Sprinkle the gelatine over 125 ml (4 fl oz/½ cup) cool water in a small saucepan. Heat through, then add the fruit juice and heat through again. Pour into a mixing bowl and leave until it begins to thicken. Stir in the yoghurt, then beat with electric beaters until fluffy.

Divide among six small dishes and refrigerate until set. If preferred, serve topped with your child's favourite fruit.

nutrition per serve: Energy 240 kJ (57 Cal); Fat 0.2 g; Saturated fat 0.04 g; Protein 5.4 g; Carbohydrate 7.9 g; Fibre 0 g; Cholesterol 2 mg

# FRUIT SALAD WITH RICOTTA YOGHURT

THIS FRESH FRUIT SALAD IS RICH IN VITAMIN C, FIBRE, POTASSIUM AND ANTIOXIDANTS, WHILE THE RICOTTA YOGHURT PROVIDES PROTEIN AND CALCIUM. THE RICOTTA YOGHURT CAN ALSO BE USED AS A DIP WITH FRESH OR TINNED FRUIT OR AS A HEALTHY ALTERNATIVE TO WHIPPED CREAM.

**500 g (1 lb 2 oz) peeled, seedless watermelon, cut into cubes**
**300 g (10½ oz) peeled rockmelon or any orange-fleshed melon, cut into cubes**
**250 g (9 oz) strawberries, hulled and cut into quarters**
**½ small pineapple, peeled and cut into pieces**
**1 small handful mint (optional)**

**SYRUP**
**125 ml (4 fl oz/½ cup) lime juice**
**45 g (1½ oz/¼ cup) soft brown sugar**
**1 tsp natural vanilla extract**

**RICOTTA YOGHURT**
**150 g (5½ oz) ricotta cheese**
**150 g (5½ oz) low-fat plain yoghurt**
**2 tsp soft brown sugar**

PREP TIME: 20 MINUTES + CHILLING
COOKING TIME: 15 MINUTES
SERVES 6

Place the fruit and mint (if using) in a bowl and mix gently.

To make the syrup, put the lime juice, brown sugar and 125 ml (4 fl oz/½ cup) water in a small saucepan and stir over low heat until the sugar dissolves. Stir in the vanilla. Bring to the boil, then reduce the heat and simmer for 10 minutes, or until the syrup has reduced and thickened.

Combine the ricotta and yoghurt in a mixing bowl and using electric beaters, beat until smooth. Add the sugar to sweeten a little.

Pour the syrup over the fruit and refrigerate until cold. Serve with the ricotta yoghurt.

nutrition per serve: Energy 924 kJ (221 Cal); Fat 4.8 g; Saturated fat 2.7 g; Protein 8.9 g; Carbohydrate 31.8 g; Fibre 4.3 g; Cholesterol 20 mg

USE A READY-MADE PASTRY MADE WITH UNSATURATED FATS SUCH AS CANOLA OIL INSTEAD OF BUTTER AND YOU GO A LONG WAY TOWARDS MAKING THIS A HEALTHIER TREAT. ASK THE KIDS TO HELP WITH DECORATING THE PASTRY WITH THE APPLE SLICES.

nutrition per serve: Energy 717 kJ (171 Cal)
Fat 7.7 g
Saturated fat 4 g
Protein 2.9 g
Carbohydrate 22.3 g
Fibre 1.7 g
Cholesterol 10 mg

# APPLE PASTRY PUFFS

**1 sheet ready-made reduced-fat**
   **puff pastry**
**milk, for brushing**
**1 apple**
**1 tsp margarine**
**2 tsp caster (superfine) sugar**
**low-fat vanilla yoghurt or custard,**
   **to serve**

PREP TIME: 15 MINUTES
COOKING TIME: 15–20 MINUTES
SERVES 4

Preheat the oven to 190°C (375°F/Gas 5). Lightly grease a baking tray. Cut the pastry into four 11 cm (4¼ in) rounds and place on the prepared tray. Brush the pastry rounds with a little milk.

Peel and core the apple and slice very thinly. Arrange the apple slices in a circular shape over each of the pastry rounds. Dot with the margarine and sprinkle with the sugar.

Bake the apple pastries for 15–20 minutes, or until the pastries are puffed and golden and the apple is tender. Serve warm with a dollop of yoghurt or custard.

# CHOC-BANANA BITES

BESIDES BEING A GOOD SOURCE OF VITAMIN C AND ENERGY-GIVING
CARBOHYDRATES, BANANAS ARE A GREAT EASY-TO-HANDLE FRUIT FOR KIDS.

**5 wooden iceblock (popsicle) sticks,
cut in half**
**3 large bananas, peeled, each cut
into 3 pieces**
**125 g (4½ oz) milk or dark cooking
chocolate, chopped**

PREP TIME: 10 MINUTES + 4 HOURS
FREEZING
COOKING TIME: 5 MINUTES
MAKES 9

Line a baking tray with foil. Carefully push a half-stick into each piece of banana. Place on the prepared tray and freeze for 2 hours, or until firm.

Put the chocolate in a small heatproof bowl. Stand the bowl over a saucepan of simmering water and stir until the chocolate has melted and is smooth.

Working with one banana piece at a time, dip each piece into the hot chocolate mixture, turning to fully coat. Drain off any excess chocolate. Place the banana pieces on the prepared tray. Refrigerate until the chocolate has set, then wrap in plastic wrap and place in the freezer for at least 2 hours to harden. Serve frozen.

nutrition per banana bite: Energy 449 kJ (107 Cal); Fat 4.1 g; Saturated fat 3.1 g; Protein 1.3 g; Carbohydrate 16.3 g; Fibre 1.3 g; Cholesterol 0.5 mg

# FROZEN FRUIT KEBABS

NEW AND UNUSUAL WAYS TO EAT FRUIT WILL ALWAYS APPEAL TO CHILDREN,
SO THESE FRUIT KEBABS SHOULD BE A HIT.

**140 g (5 oz) peeled pineapple**
**½ mango**
**80 g (2¾ oz) peeled, seedless watermelon**
**100 g (3½ oz) peeled rockmelon or any**
**orange-fleshed melon**
**4 wooden iceblock (popsicle) sticks**

PREP TIME: 1O MINUTES + 4 HOURS
FREEZING
COOKING TIME: NIL
MAKES 4

Cut each fruit into four cubes. Thread the cubes onto the wooden sticks and freeze for 4 hours, or until frozen.

To serve, remove the fruit sticks from the freezer 10 minutes before eating to allow them to soften slightly.

HINT:
• You can make extra quantities of this recipe and keep in the freezer for a hot day.

nutrition per fruit kebab: Energy 170 kJ (41 Cal); Fat 0.1 g; Saturated fat 0 g; Protein 0.8 g; Carbohydrate 8.2 g; Fibre 1.5 g; Cholesterol 0 mg

# ORANGE SORBET

**10–12 oranges**
**90 g (3¼ oz/¾ cup) icing (confectioners')**
   **sugar**
**2 tbsp lemon juice**

PREP TIME: 20 MINUTES + FREEZING

COOKING TIME: NIL

SERVES 6

Cut the oranges in half and carefully squeeze out the juice, taking care not to damage the skins. Dissolve the icing sugar in the orange juice, add the lemon juice and pour into a freezer container. Cover the surface with baking paper and freeze for 1 hour.

Scrape the remaining flesh and membrane out of six of the orange halves, then cover the orange skins with plastic wrap and refrigerate.

After 1 hour, stir any ice crystals that have formed around the edge of the sorbet back into the centre and return to the freezer. Repeat every hour, or until nearly frozen, then leave to freeze overnight.

Divide the sorbet among the orange skins and freeze until ready to serve. The sorbet may seem very hard when it has frozen overnight but it will melt quickly, so work fast. Serve the sorbet in the orange skins.

THIS LIGHT AND REFRESHING
LOW-FAT DESSERT IS PERFECT
FOR SUMMER WHEN SOMETHING
COOL AND ICY IS ALWAYS A TREAT.

nutrition per serve: Energy 465 kJ (111 Cal)
Fat 0.2 g
Saturated fat 0 g
Protein 0.8 g
Carbohydrate 26.6 g
Fibre 0.2 g
Cholesterol 0 mg

# MANGO CITRUS SAUCE

BURSTING WITH THE VITAMINS OF YELLOW FRUIT, BETA-CAROTENE AND
VITAMIN C, THIS SAUCE EVEN HAS A LITTLE FIBRE, MAKING IT A MUCH
HEALTHIER ALTERNATIVE TO WHAT YOU'D BUY IN A BOTTLE.

**300 g (10½ oz) chopped mango (you will
   need 1 mango)**
**80 ml (2½ fl oz/⅓ cup) orange juice**
**1 lime, juiced**
**1–2 tbsp icing (confectioners') sugar**
**low-fat vanilla yoghurt, to serve**

PREP TIME: 10 MINUTES
COOKING TIME: NIL
SERVES 6

Combine the mango, orange juice and lime juice in a food processor. Process until the
mixture is smooth. Sweeten to taste with icing sugar, if needed.

Serve over yoghurt or ice cream, or as a sauce over plain pancakes or waffles. Store for
2 days in the refrigerator.

HINT:
• You can make this recipe using other fresh stone fruit, such as peaches or nectarines.

nutrition per serve: Energy 197 kJ (47 Cal); Fat 0.1 g; Saturated fat 0 g; Protein 0.7 g;
Carbohydrate 10.2 g; Fibre 0.8 g; Cholesterol 0 mg

# GRILLED MAPLE BANANAS WITH BLUEBERRIES

YOUR CHILDREN DON'T NEED TO EAT DESSERT EVERY NIGHT, BUT WHEN THEY DO, A FRUIT-BASED ONE LIKE THIS GOES A LONG WAY TOWARDS FURTHERING THEIR DAY'S NUTRITION.

**4 sugar or finger bananas**
**2 tbsp soft brown sugar**
**25 g (1 oz) margarine, melted**
**1 tbsp orange juice**
**fresh blueberries, to serve**
**80 ml (2½ fl oz/⅓ cup) maple syrup**

PREP TIME: 10 MINUTES
COOKING TIME: 3 MINUTES
SERVES 4

Preheat a barbecue grill plate or flatplate to medium. Peel the bananas and cut them in half lengthways. Put the sugar, margarine and orange juice in a small bowl and mix well until the sugar has dissolved. Brush the mixture evenly over the bananas on all sides.

Lightly brush the barbecue plate with oil and cook the bananas for 2–3 minutes, or until the bananas are tender and browned.

Place the bananas on serving plates and sprinkle with blueberries. Drizzle with the maple syrup and serve.

nutrition per serve: Energy 1135 kJ (271 Cal); Fat 4.5 g; Saturated fat 0.8 g; Protein 1.8 g; Carbohydrate 54.9 g; Fibre 4.4 g; Cholesterol 0 mg

APPLES ARE A GOOD SOURCE OF
LOW-GI CARBOHYDRATES AND
THE HEALTH PROTECTING
PHYTOCHEMICALS KNOWN AS
FLAVONOIDS. FOR MORE FIBRE,
THINLY SLICE THE APPLES,
LEAVING THE SKIN ON.

nutrition per serve: Energy 1360 kJ (325 Cal)
Fat 7.7 g
Saturated fat 0.7 g
Protein 6.3 g
Carbohydrate 56.7 g
Fibre 5.5 g
Cholesterol 0 mg

# APPLE CRUMBLE

6 granny smith apples, peeled, cored
  and chopped
55 g (2 oz/¼ cup) sugar
30 g (1 oz/¼ cup) sultanas (golden raisins)
1 tbsp cornflour (cornstarch)
140 g (5 oz/1⅓ cups) traditional rolled
  (porridge) oats
1 tbsp soft brown sugar
60 g (2¼ oz/½ cup) slivered almonds

2 tbsp honey
2 egg whites
low-fat custard or ice cream,
  to serve

PREP TIME: 15 MINUTES
COOKING TIME: 35 MINUTES
SERVES 6

Preheat the oven to 180°C (350°F/Gas 4). Place the apples in a saucepan with the sugar and 185 ml (6 fl oz/¾ cup) water. Cook, covered, over low heat for 6 minutes, or until just tender. Add the sultanas and cook for a further 2 minutes.

Mix the cornflour with 1 tablespoon cold water, add to the pan and cook for 1 minute, or until thickened. Spoon into six 250 ml (9 fl oz/1 cup) ramekins.

Place the oats, brown sugar, almonds, honey and egg whites in a bowl and mix until well combined and lumps form. Divide among the ramekins to cover the apple mixture. Bake the crumble for 20–25 minutes, or until the tops are golden brown and crunchy. Serve with the custard or ice cream.

# BREAD AND BUTTER PUDDING

THIS IS A WHOLESOME TREAT BASED ON BREAD, MILK, EGGS AND FRUIT. THE
PUDDING IS MADE MORE NUTRITIOUS WITH THE USE OF WHOLEMEAL BREAD,
BUT CAN BE MADE EVEN MORE SO WITH EVEN HIGHER FIBRE VARIETIES,
SUCH AS WHOLEGRAIN.

**6 slices wholemeal (whole-wheat) bread**
**20 g (¾ oz) margarine**
**750 ml (26 fl oz/3 cups) reduced-fat milk**
**¼ tsp grated lemon zest**
**110 g (3¾ oz/½ cup) sugar**
**4 eggs**
**125 g (4½ oz/¾ cup) mixed dried fruit**

PREP TIME: 20 MINUTES + 10 MINUTES
STANDING
COOKING TIME: 35 MINUTES
SERVES 4

Preheat the oven to 180°C (350°F/Gas 4). Grease an ovenproof dish. Remove the crusts
and spread the bread with the margarine.

Heat the milk in a saucepan and add the lemon zest. Bring to the boil, then cover and
remove from the heat, leaving to infuse for 10 minutes. Beat the sugar and eggs together,
then strain the milk over the eggs and mix well.

Scatter half the dried fruit over the bottom of the prepared dish and arrange the bread,
margarine side down, on top. Pour in half the custard, then repeat with the remaining fruit,
bread and custard. Place the dish in a baking tin and add enough water to fill halfway up
the outside of the dish. Bake for 35 minutes. Serve with low-fat ice cream if desired.

nutrition per serve: Energy 1988 kJ (475 Cal); Fat 12.6 g; Saturated fat 4.1 g; Protein 18.1 g;
Carbohydrate 72.8 g; Fibre 4.1 g; Cholesterol 201 mg

# CHOCOLATE AND ORANGE SELF-SAUCING PUDDINGS

SOME DESSERTS ARE JUST MEANT TO TASTE GREAT RATHER THAN BE SUPER HEALTHY. MAKING THIS YOURSELF, HOWEVER, WILL MEAN YOUR CHILDREN WON'T GET THE ADDITIVES, PRESERVATIVES AND COLOURS THEY WOULD IF YOU MADE IT FROM A PACKET.

2 tbsp unsweetened cocoa powder
125 g (4½ oz/1 cup) self-raising flour
60 g (2¼ oz) light cream cheese
1 tsp finely grated orange zest
115 g (4 oz/½ cup) caster (superfine) sugar
125 ml (4 fl oz/½ cup) reduced-fat milk
80 ml (2½ fl oz/⅓ cup) orange juice

95 g (3¼ oz/½ cup) soft brown sugar
1 tbsp unsweetened cocoa powder, extra
icing (confectioners') sugar, to dust

PREP TIME: 15 MINUTES
COOKING TIME: 35 MINUTES
SERVES 4

Preheat the oven to 180°C (350°F/Gas 4). Sift the cocoa powder with the flour, at least twice. Using a wooden spoon, blend the cream cheese, orange zest and caster sugar until smooth.

Fold the flour mixture and milk alternately into the cream cheese mixture and stir in the orange juice. Pour the mixture into four greased 310 ml (10¾ fl oz/1¼ cup) ramekins.

Combine the brown sugar and extra cocoa and sprinkle evenly over the surface of the puddings. Carefully pour 80 ml (2½ fl oz/⅓ cup) boiling water over the back of a spoon onto each pudding. Place on a baking tray and bake for 35 minutes, or until firm. Dust with icing sugar and serve.

nutrition per serve: Energy 1691 kJ (404 Cal); Fat 5.7 g; Saturated fat 3.5 g; Protein 7.6 g; Carbohydrate 81.9 g; Fibre 1.5 g; Cholesterol 15 mg

# RICE PUDDING

**110 g (3¾ oz/½ cup) risotto rice**
**1 litre (35 fl oz/4 cups) reduced-fat milk**
**30 g (1 oz/¼ cup) sultanas (golden
   raisins)**
**2 tbsp caster (superfine) sugar**
**1 tsp natural vanilla extract**

**pinch of ground cinnamon**
**fresh berries, to garnish (optional)**

PREP TIME: 10 MINUTES
COOKING TIME: 1½ HOURS
SERVES 4

Preheat the oven to 180°C (350°F/Gas 4).

Place the rice, milk, sultanas, sugar, vanilla and cinnamon in a 1.5 litre (52 fl oz/6 cup) capacity baking dish and stir to combine.

Bake for about 1½ hours, stirring every 15 minutes for the first hour to make sure the rice doesn't stick to the dish. Remove the pudding from the oven when it has the consistency of creamed rice. Do not overcook or it may dry out. Cool slightly and top with fresh berries if desired.

GOOD RICE PUDDING TAKES TIME TO COOK, ALTHOUGH IT'S VERY EASY TO PREPARE. THE SULTANAS ADD EXTRA SWEETNESS AND FIBRE, BUT YOU CAN LEAVE THEM OUT IF YOU PREFER.

nutrition per serve: Energy 1176 kJ (281 Cal)
Fat 3.8 g
Saturated fat 2.3 g
Protein 12 g
Carbohydrate 49.4 g
Fibre 0.5 g
Cholesterol 18 mg

## USEFUL CONTACTS

If having read the information in this book you'd like to know more, look at these helpful websites:

### General healthy eating information and fact sheets

Go For Your Life
www.goforyourlife.vic.gov.au

UK Food Standards Agency's
consumer site
www.eatwell.gov.uk

Healthy kids
www.healthykids.nsw.gov.au

Kids' Health
www.kidshealth.org

My pyramid
www.mypyramid.gov

Fruits and Veggies More Matters
www.fruitsandveggiesmorematters.org

Food For Kids
www.choicefoodforkids.com.au

### Getting families active

Active Healthy Kids Canada
www.activehealthykids.ca

Be active
www.beactive.com.au

Go Kids
www.gokids.org.nz

### Growth and weight issues

National Center for Health Statistics
www.cdc.gov/growthcharts/

National Obesity Forum
www.nationalobesityforum.org.uk

Kids Weigh In
www.kidsweighin.org

Way to go Weigh to Grow
www.healthyweightforkids.org

# INDEX

Entries in *italics* are topics; all the other entries are recipes.

**190**

**191**